THE JOURNAL OF
CORPORATE CITIZENSHIP

Issue 56
December 2014

Theme Issue: **Japanese Approaches to CSR**

Edited by Kanji Tanimoto,
Waseda University, Japan

ISBN: 978-1-78353-263-6

print ISSN 1470-5001   *online* ISSN 2051-4700

ISBN 978-1-78353-263-6

Greenleaf
PUBLISHING

THE JOURNAL OF CORPORATE CITIZENSHIP

General Editor Malcolm McIntosh,
Asia-Pacific Centre for Sustainable Enterprise, Griffith Business School, Australia

Regional Editor *North America*: Professor Sandra Waddock, Boston College, Carroll School of Management, USA

Publisher Rebecca Macklin, Greenleaf Publishing, UK   **Assistant Publisher** Anna Comerford, Greenleaf Publishing, UK

Production Editor Sadie Gornall-Jones, Greenleaf Publishing, UK

CORRESPONDENCE

The Journal of Corporate Citizenship encourages response from its readers to any of the issues raised in the journal. All correspondence is welcomed and should be sent to the General Editor c/o Greenleaf Publishing, Aizlewood's Mill, Nursery St, Sheffield S3 8GG, UK; jcc@greenleaf-publishing.com.

All content should be submitted via **online submission**. For more information see the journal homepage at www.greenleaf-publishing.com/jcc.

Books to be considered for review should be marked for the attention of the Book Review Editor c/o Greenleaf Publishing, Aizlewood's Mill, Nursery St, Sheffield S3 8GG, UK; jcc@greenleaf-publishing.com.

• All articles published in *The Journal of Corporate Citizenship* are assessed by an external panel of business professionals, consultants and academics.

• *The Journal of Corporate Citizenship* is indexed with and included in: **Cabells, EBSCO, ProQuest, Gale, ABDC** and **Journalseek.net**. It is monitored by 'Political Science and Government Abstracts' and 'Sociological Abstracts'.

SUBSCRIPTION RATES

The Journal of Corporate Citizenship is a quarterly journal, appearing in March, June, September and December of each year. Cheques should be made payable to Greenleaf Publishing and sent to the address below.

Annual online subscription
Individuals: £80.00/€112.50/US$150.00
Organizations: £540.00/€650.00/US$850.00

Annual print and online subscription
Individuals: £90.00/€120.00/US$160.00
Organizations: £550.00/€672.50/US$860.00

Annual print subscription
Individuals: £80.00/€112.50/US$150.00
Organizations: £180.00/€240.00/US$320.00

The Journal of Corporate Citizenship
Greenleaf Publishing Ltd, Aizlewood Business Centre, Aizlewood's Mill, Nursery Street, Sheffield S3 8GG, UK
Tel: +44 (0)114 282 3475   Fax: +44 (0)114 282 3476   Email: jcc@greenleaf-publishing.com.
Or order from our website: www.greenleaf-publishing.com/jcc.

ADVERTISING

The Journal of Corporate Citizenship will accept a strictly limited amount of display advertising in future issues. It is also possible to book inserts. Suitable material for promotion includes publications, conferences and consulting services. For details on rates and availability, please email jcc@greenleaf-publishing.com.

FSC
www.fsc.org
MIX
Paper from
responsible sources
FSC® C013604

Printed in the UK on environmentally friendly, acid-free paper from managed forests by CPI Group (UK) Ltd, Croydon

Editorial

Issue 56 *December 2014*

Malcolm McIntosh

General Editor, Journal of Corporate Citizenship

IT IS OFTEN THE CASE THAT *JCC*'S SPECIAL issues have attracted significant attention and have been cited more often years later because they offer a window into other worlds for our global readership. I hope this is the case with this significant issue on Japanese CSR, edited by Kanji Tanimoto.

I admit to having had a love affair with Japan since I first taught there in the late 1970s. I have kept returning regularly and am now associated with Doshisha Business School and its radical Global MBA programme.

I have argued elsewhere that much corporate social responsibility and corporate citizenship theory and action is part of the neoliberal push, trying to ameliorate the downside of a rapacious model of capitalism that Adam Smith would not have recognised. But this is only true when viewed as an adjunct to the American and European models of business and capitalism. As Kanji Tanimoto says in his introduction to this special issue of *JCC*, the 'stakeholder model' is not Japanese CSR because the Japanese have a consensual approach to politics and corporate governance as centrepieces of their culture. In other words, they have adopted many aspects of Western governance codes, but, as with every import, they have had their own ways of doing things and so have 'Japanised' these imports.

Many people who have not visited Japan and who have not studied its exceptional culture may see it as part of the Asian milieu. Of course, it is part of Asia geographically and historically, but it is unique in many ways, and very different from much of the rest of Asia. Indeed, the idea of Asia, and 'Asian values', as one whole is not as simple as is often suggested.

Japan's separation from the world for 250 years until Admiral Perry's trade-or-we-will-destroy-you threat in 1856 gave it a resilience unknown elsewhere in the world, even now. Its entry into the Second World War and imperialist pretensions were partly driven by pressure from the US to trade and its comparative lack of raw materials, particularly oil. How it behaved in the 1930s and '40s is to its long-lasting shame and it is dealing with the consequences of its behaviour, and its denial, 80 years later. It is also trying to deal with its embedded misogyny and there are efforts to get more women into the workforce, although it will be a long time until they make it into the boardroom or into government.

Japanese corporations, who are part of all our daily lives, should be able to help civilise parochial right-wing nationalist politics. This is an issue not just for Japan but for international governance. Governments are exposed to democratic, or stakeholder, scrutiny far more than our global corporations. This is as true for Sony and Toyota as it is for US Ford, the UK's Barclays, Australia's BHP Billiton, China's Sinopec and India's Adani.

Japan has an aesthetic and a spirit that is unique and I would encourage everyone to visit and wonder, not least because of the beauty and the wonderful food, but also to ask the question: 'where does Japan go now?' It led the way in post-war economic growth but managed to remain one of the most egalitarian countries in the world, to develop a fully inclusive national health system that works day-to-day, but with one of the lowest tax rates in the world. By many countries' standards, it is peaceful and almost crime-free. And as the world's third largest economy its comparatively low per capita carbon emissions put some others to shame.

Thank you, Kanji, for this issue and to all those who proffered papers.

Malcolm McIntosh
Bath, England
December 2014

DOI: [10.9774/GLEAF.8757.2014.de.00001]

Introduction

Japanese Approaches to CSR

Issue 56 *December 2014*

Kanji Tanimoto
Waseda University, Japan

CSR and Management in Japan

HOW IS CORPORATE SOCIAL RESPONSIBILITY (CSR) understood and managed in Japanese business and how is it part of 'good' corporate governance? A joint conference on this theme was held in September 2013 by the Japan Forum of Business and Society[1] (JFBS: an academic association in Japan, founded in 2011) and the Humboldt University International CSR Conference,[2] in cooperation with the Japanese German Center Berlin (JDZB). The major topics discussed were the relationship between CSR management and corporate governance, and Japanese approaches to CSR management from various academic and practical perspectives. For details, refer to JFBS (2014).

The discussion on CSR has grown rapidly and internationally over the last two decades in both business and academic communities, and during the past decade the debate has also spread to and throughout Japan. The current CSR movement has been developed in European and Anglo-American contexts, based on principles of market, industrial, business and social structures. However, CSR has also taken root in other countries and regions, including Japan, and the development of CSR is at different stages throughout these territories (Welford, 2005; Matten and Moon, 2008; Higgins and Debroux, 2009; Mallin, 2009, Fukukawa, 2009, Mermod and Idowu, 2014). Japanese companies have also been influenced by this global movement, learning about CSR and translating it into the Japanese context (Suzuki, Tanimoto and Kokko, 2010; Amoun, Jaussand and Matinez, 2012; Fukukwa and Mongran, 2013, Tanimoto, 2013). This growing awareness of CSR has prompted Japanese corporations to change certain aspects of corporate policy in order to improve relations with stakeholders.

Traditionally, the Japanese economic system has been structured by relational trading between firms, relational banking, and long-term relationships between the company and its employees (Dore, 2000). Since the end of World War II, Japanese

---

1 http://j-fbs.jp/
2 www.csr-hu-berlin.org/

corporations have tended to forge close relationships with core stakeholders, namely major corporate shareholders, permanent employees, primary subcontractors and the government. The corporation and its core stakeholders have formed a 'closed network' in market society. They have shared values and common goals toward economic development; a stable, lasting and closed relationship with core stakeholders has thus been constructed. On the other hand, peripheral stakeholders have been excluded from the system. This typical system, adopted by most Japanese corporations, has been described as a 'stakeholder model', but it is not a model based on any notion of CSR (Tanimoto, 2009). Still, the system containing this model has undoubtedly been one of the great strengths of the Japanese economy. It is necessary, however, to explore whether this system remains a strength or has become, rather, a weakness for Japanese corporations, as well as to consider how the business environment in Japan is changing in today's globalised economy. There is also a need to determine how Japan's corporations have tackled the issue of CSR and embedded it into Japanese corporate society.

Research issues

There is much debate about how to incorporate the concept and philosophy of CSR into the contexts of different countries. Since the early 2000s, there have been a growing number of studies offering alternative perspectives on CSR, deriving from Asia and other regions outside of Europe and North America. What is important, however, is the examination of how CSR management and practical wisdom in organisations works in diverse countries and regions, rather than just the exercise of highlighting the cultural differences among those regions.

This special issue of the *Journal of Corporate Citizenship* focuses on and analyses the uniqueness of Japanese industrial and organisational structures, as well as the distinct social and cultural contexts which contain them. Japanese companies are finding that CSR is a crucial issue in daily business management and global business strategy. Pressure from the global CSR movement has driven the CSR boom in Japan since the early 2000s, although many Japanese corporations at first hesitated to respond. One issue is that there is no common understanding of what comprises global CSR standards or of which CSR policies are best for Japanese corporations. As a result, most Japanese companies do what other companies are doing, keeping their CSR activities to the minimum requirements. This leads to stronger mimicry; institutional isomorphism begins to occur in CSR management.

CSR management in Japan has rapidly institutionalised since around the mid-2000s. Data from Toyo Keizai (2013) shows that 73.2% of companies surveyed have established a CSR department, 65.8% have a CSR executive in place, and 57.2% produce documentation on CSR policy. Japan has been ranked among the leading countries in the world in terms of publishing CSR reports over the last decade (KPMG, 2011). However, it must be noted that CSR management does not automatically begin to function adequately in an organisation through the simple act of establishing a CSR institution. It is important to discuss how managers in every department have learned about and have interpreted global CSR standards and norms in organisational contexts, and also how CSR managers in Japan choose to transmit CSR policies to local contexts.

Clearly, CSR should be incorporated into management processes and corporate governance (Jamali, Safieddine and Rabbath, 2008; Devinney, Schwalbach and Williams, 2013), and it needs to be an integral part of management strategy and business planning. Japanese corporations have come to learn that it is important to meet the expectations and earn the trust of their stakeholders. Executives need to govern the management process, responding to the voices and interests of relevant stakeholders (Bhattacharya, 2011). Furthermore, in the face of global competition, Japanese corporations have found it necessary to advance their activities in environmentally and socially responsible business which contributes to sustainable development in both local and global communities (Laszlo and Zhexembayeva, 2011; Regeneration Project, 2012; Williams, 2014) .

There are some crucial questions to be asked in Japanese corporations. In response to global pressure from the CSR movement, how have and how should Japanese companies import the concept of CSR and integrate it into management systems and strategy? In recent years, Japanese corporations have increasingly been embedding a new management concept, originating in Western business practice, into traditional Japanese business values. In the same way, how do and how should they translate CSR and incorporate it into governance systems and engagement with stakeholders? What are the well-developed and under-developed points, respectively, of current CSR management in Japanese corporations? Has the rapid institutionalisation of CSR in Japan meant that existing CSR management systems currently function well? And when advancing into overseas markets, how do and how should Japanese companies manage CSR polices in their overseas subsidiaries? The traditional themes of the internationalisation and localisation of management systems, which have been widely discussed in the field of international management, are also points of focus in relation to CSR management abroad. Finally, what will be the next strategic challenge for Japanese corporations in the journey towards sustainable development?

In this special issue

The call for papers for this special issue of the *JCC* intended to explore the Japanese approaches to CSR. The call for papers attracted 17 submissions over a relatively short period. The submissions came from across the world and a variety of topics were discussed. Through the usual process of double-blind peer review, four papers were finally selected.

This special issue of *JCC* will discuss how Japanese corporations respond to the CSR movement, the extent to which they embed CSR in management processes, and how they diffuse CSR policy throughout their overseas subsidiaries. It will also analyse the challenges corporations are facing in ensuring CSR systems function within their organisations and in contributing to global sustainable development. The articles have a particular focus on Japanese and global CSR issues and the challenges they pose to corporations.

The issue begins with a paper written by Richard E. Wokutch, entitled 'Corporate Social Responsibility, Japanese Style, Revisited'. The study describes the nature of CSR thinking in Japan through an analysis of traditional labour relations, how these have transited over time, and two opposing evaluations of the Japanese employment system. He argues that the interests of core stakeholders are favoured over those of other stakeholders, but also that the traditional relationship with stakeholders has been changed by the introduction of CSR policy.

The second paper, written by Patrick Albrecht and Christopher Greenwald, of PwC and Rebecon SAM, respectively, is entitled 'Financial Materiality of Sustainability: The Japanese Context'. They analyse the present situation of sustainability initiatives in Japanese corporations, based on Dow Jones Sustainability Index data. They suggest that environmental initiatives and social initiatives should be mainstreamed into core strategic decision-making processes, but question how that can be achieved in reality. They further examine the strengths and weaknesses of sustainability management within Japanese companies, and highlight a number of particular challenges.

The third paper, written by Carol Reade, Koichi Goka, Robbin Thorp, Masahiro Mitsuhata and Marius Wasbauer, is entitled 'CSR, Biodiversity, and Japan's Stakeholder Approach to the Global Bumble Bee Trade'. They explore the question of how to protect biodiversity while meeting commercial interests as a CSR challenge. They identify a unique Japanese case and describe the importance of a stakeholder approach in the efforts to protect local species from alien species, based on what is called the precautionary principle. They highlight the importance of collaboration among relevant stakeholders—the scientific community, government, and business—in the process of setting up an acceptable rule.

The fourth paper, written by Roger Levermore, is entitled 'Organisational Geographies and Corporate Responsibility: A Case Study of Japanese Multinational Corporations Operating in South Africa and Tanzania'. Here, the author discusses how multinational corporations (MNCs) choose to adopt CSR polices in subsidiaries located in advancing overseas markets, considering how CSR strategy is influenced by organisational geographies. He examines seven case studies of Japanese MNCs subsidiaries, looking at how CSR strategic management was shaped in each, and uses this evidence to categorise the various approaches taken into five types. The paper is therefore an exploration of the geographical and organisational influences which shape the strategic approach taken to CSR by Japanese MNCs in their global operations.

These four unique papers discuss various aspects of the Japanese approach to CSR management. This special issue intends to shine a light on the current CSR situation of Japanese companies, as well as to identify some of the key challenges faced in the processes of embedding CSR into management systems and of operating CSR practices in international contexts.

References

Amann, B., Jaussaud, J. and Martinez, I. (2012). 'Corporate social responsibility in Japan: Family and non-family business differences and determinants', *Asian Business and Management*, 11(3): 329-345.

Bhattacharya, C.B., Sen, S. and Korschun, D. (2011). *Leveraging Corporate Responsibility*, Cambridge University Press, Cambridge.

Devinney, T.M., Schwalbach, J. and Williams, C.A. (2013). 'Corporate Social Responsibility and Corporate Governance: Comparative Perspectives' Special Issue: Corporate Social Responsibility, Institutional Structures and Corporate Governance, *Corporate Governance: An International Review*, 21(5): 413-419.

Dore, R. (2000). *Stock Market Capitalism: Welfare Capitalism—Japan and Germany versus Anglo-Saxons*, Oxford University Press, Oxford.

Fukukawa, K. ed. (2009). *Corporate Social Responsibility in Asia*, Routledge, Abingdon.

Fukukawa, K. and S. Manghani (2013). 'Transformations and Translations of Japanese Business and Society: A Retrospective', in M. McIntosh (ed.), *The Necessary Transition: Transition and Transformation Issues in the Journey towards the Sustainable Enterprise Economy*, Greenleaf Publishing, Sheffield, UK, pp.80-97.

Higgins, C. and Debroux, P. (2009). 'Globalization and CSR in Asia', *Asian Business and Management*, 8(2): 125-127.

Jamali, D., Safieddine, A.M. and Rabbath, M. (2008). 'Corporate Governance and Corporate Social Responsibility Synergies and Interrelationships', *Corporate Governance: An International Review*, 16(5): 443-459.

JFBS ed. (2014). *CSR and Corporate Governance*, Chikura Shobo, Tokyo.

KPMG (2011). KPMG International Survey of Corporate Responsibility Reporting 2011.

Laszlo, C. and Zhexembayeva, N. (2011). *Embedded Sustainability*, Greenleaf Publishing, Sheffield.

Mallin, C.A. (ed.) (2009). *Corporate Social Responsibility: A Case Study Approach*, Edward Elgar Publishing, Cheltenham.

Matten, D. and Moon, J. (2008). 'Implicit and Explicit CSR: A Conceptual Framework for a Comparative Understanding of Corporate Social Responsibility', *Academy of Management Review*, 33(2): 404-424.

Mermod, A.Y. and Idowu, S.O. (eds.) (2014). *Corporate Social Responsibility in the Global Business World*, Springer, Heidelberg.

Regeneration Project (2012). *Unfinished Business, Perspectives from the Sustainable Development Frontier*, GlobeScan and SustainAbility.

Suzuki, K. Tanimoto, K. and Kokko, A. (2010). 'Does Foreign Investment Matter? The Effects of Foreign Investment on the Institutionalization of Corporate Social Responsibility by Japanese Firms', *Asian Business & Management*, 9(3): 379-400.

Tanimoto, K. (2009). 'Structural Change in Corporate Society and CSR in Japan', Fukukawa, K. (ed.), *Corporate Social Responsibility in Asia*, Routledge, Abingdon, pp.45-65.

Tanimoto, K. (2013). 'Corporate Social Responsibility and Management Process in Japanese Corporations', *World Review of Entrepreneurship, Management and Sustainable Development*, 9(1): 10-25.

Welford, R. (2005). 'Corporate Social responsibility in Europe, North America and Asia', *Journal of Corporate Citizenship*, 17: 33-52.

Williams, O.F. (2014). 'CSR: Will it Change the World? Hope for the Future: An Emerging Logic in Business Practice', *Journal of Corporate Citizenship*, 53: 9-26.

Kanji Tanimoto is a Professor in Business and Society at the School of Commerce, Waseda University. He is a Visiting Professor at the Free University of Berlin in 2010 and 2014. He is a founder and a president of an academy in Japan: Japan Forum of Business and Society. His research interests are Business and Society, Corporate Social Responsibility, Social Business and Social Innovation.

✉ School of Commerce, Waseda University, 1-6-1, Nishi-Waseda, Shinjyuku-Ku, Tokyo, 169-8050, Japan

🖥 k.tanimoto@tanimoto-office.jp

🌐 http://tanimoto-office.jp/

DOI: [10.9774/GLEAF.8757.2014.de.00002]

Corporate Social Responsibility Japanese Style, Revisited*

Richard E. Wokutch
Virginia Tech, USA

This paper provides a long-term perspective on the way in which corporate social responsibility (CSR) has been thought of and managed in Japan over approximately the last 30 years. Although dealing with a wide range of social concerns the paper pays particular attention to the handling of an issue, worker safety and health, which has been the subject of considerable contentiousness in the USA. Special emphasis is placed on describing: 1) the positive and negative stereotypes of CSR in Japan and how both have elements of truth in them; 2) the underlying motivations and determinants of CSR in Japan that dictate the distinctive Japanese manner of thinking about and practising CSR; 3) how CSR practices and the thinking about CSR have changed over this period; and 4) the reasons for these changes.

- Japan
- Corporate social responsibility
- Business ethics
- Worker safety and health
- Karoshi
- Fukushima
- Tsunami

Richard E. Wokutch is Pamplin Professor of Management at Virginia Tech. His research focuses on international business ethics and his publications include, *Worker Protection, Japanese Style*, published by Cornell University Press and *Rising Above Sweatshops* (Praeger). He has also published in journals such as *California Management Review, Academy of Management Executive, Business Ethics Quarterly, and Business & Society*. A past chair of the Social Issues in Management Division of the Academy of Management, he was a recipient of its Sumner Marcus Award, Fulbright Research fellowships to Germany and Japan, and the Virginia Tech Alumni Award for Outstanding International Research.

Department of Management (0233), 2017 Pamplin Hall, Virginia Tech, Blacksburg, VA 24061, USA

wokutch@vt.edu

* The author would like to acknowledge the support of the Japan Fulbright Program which was indispensable in this research. I would also like to express my sincere gratitude to Professor Mitsuhiro Umezu and Keio University for their generous assistance and hospitality. I am also very grateful to Professor Akira Saito and other members of JABES for their support in this work. Further thanks go to representatives of the many other organizations mentioned in this paper for their cooperation and assistance.

ORPORATE SOCIAL RESPONSIBILITY (CSR) PRACTICES in Japan have over the years been characterised in contradictory and extreme ways—both starkly negative and extremely laudatory. Interestingly, depending on which practices one chooses to look at there is plenty of evidence to support both of these extreme perspectives, which I have referred to elsewhere as stereotypes or myths (Wokutch, 1990b, 1992a, b).

Nowhere are these extremes more evident than in the characterisations of Japanese approaches to CSR with respect to workers. On the one hand, much of Japanese economic success has been attributed to favourable treatment of workers. According to this perspective, pleasant working conditions, lifetime employment, worker participation in decision-making (especially through the *kaizen* or continuous improvement process), company-sponsored vacations and other social activities and generally paternalistic practices make work a relatively pleasant and extremely productive experience virtually every day (Ouchi, 1981; Pascale and Athos, 1981; Schonberger, 1982). I have in the past characterised this view as the 'Myth of the Japanese Workers, Paradise' (Wokutch, 1992a, b).

On the other hand, international companies and workers competing with Japanese firms have often attributed Japanese economic success to an overworked and underpaid Japanese workforce (Fucini and Fucini, 1990; Kamata, 1982; Kazuo, 1991; Sethi *et al.*, 1984). The long working hours and after-hours social obligations of Japanese managers are also the subject of notoriety. In addition, the treatment of foreign workers, part-time and seasonal workers, and female workers has been criticised by many critics such as those noted above, leading to what I call the 'Myth of the Abused Japanese Worker' (Wokutch, 1992a, b).

In other CSR domains there have been equally contradictory accounts of Japanese corporate social performance. For example in the area of environmental protection Japanese automakers have historically led the way in fuel efficiency. In recent years, companies such as Toyota with the Prius and Honda with the Leaf have been leaders in the production of low-polluting, highly fuel-efficient vehicles. At the same time however Japan has had a spotted record on other environmental issues. In an early book, Margaret McKean (1981) detailed a number of environmental disasters and generally poor concern for the environment displayed by Japanese companies and government regulators. She also noted how the victims of environmental accidents have often been looked down upon and shunned by other members of society. With its small land mass and high population density, Japan continues to experience serious environmental problems on a day-to-day basis, but some issues are particularly noticeable. For example, in recent years Japan has been at odds with much of the rest of the world over its continued whaling operations for 'scientific purposes'. And of course the meltdown of the nuclear reactors at Fukushima, the worst nuclear disaster since Chernobyl, has been a source of continuing concern in Japan and abroad.

In this paper I will: 1) explore the conceptualisation and operationalisation of CSR in Japan through the handling of a corporate social issue, worker safety and health, that has proven particularly contentious in the USA; 2) describe the underlying motivations and determinants of CSR in Japan that dictate the characteristic Japanese way of thinking about and practising CSR; 3) explain through these underlying motivations how both the negative and positive stereotypes of CSR in Japan have components of truth in them; and 4) document how CSR practices and the thinking about CSR have changed since I started studying this issue almost 30 years ago, and attempt to explain the reasons for these changes.

Research approach and background

In the fall of 1986, I had the opportunity to study CSR in the Japanese auto industry with the support of a Fulbright Fellowship funded by a Japanese auto firm. The specific CSR issue I focused on was occupational safety and health (OSH),[1] an issue for which there are obvious benefits to be derived from labour–management cooperation, yet an often highly contentious issue in labour–management relations in the USA. I had already studied this issue in the United States, Europe, and a developing country, Kenya. So Japan, which in the mid-1980s had become the largest auto-producing country in the world, was an obvious next choice in this research stream. Though my focus was on OSH, I had the opportunity while conducting this research to observe and discuss managerial responses to a great many other social issues. My ability to observe the evolution of CSR in Japan was augmented by the fact that, beginning in 1995, I led eight different university summer study abroad programmes to Japan with a focus on CSR. These programmes involved meetings with Japanese and American managers of Japanese and American companies, governmental, and non-profit organisations operating in Japan and, at many of the companies, tours of production facilities. Most recently, while on sabbatical in the fall of 2011, I had the opportunity, 25 years later, to revisit my earlier research on OSH and other CSR issues in Japan. This follow-up research took place only months after the Great East Japanese Earthquake and the resulting tsunami and nuclear reactor meltdown at TEPCO's Fukushima Daiichi plant. Thus discussion of how these events (collectively known as '3/11') affected operations of the firms I visited figured prominently in these interviews. During the interviews we also discussed relief efforts the companies engaged in to assist members of their corporate families and others in the most severely affected areas and how these activities fit in with the companies' views of CSR.

The Fulbright Program has many very distinguished alumni in Japan, and a Fulbright Fellowship is held in considerably higher regard in that country than

---

1 Many companies I studied now also include environmental management in the same department as occupational safety and health, as these are all interrelated issues and functions. Such firms now often refer to 'SHE' or safety, health and environmental operations; however for the sake of consistency I am using here the terminology I originally used when I started this research, but with the understanding that environmental issues are also relevant.

in the United States. (By way of example, the Emperor and Empress of Japan honoured the Program with their attendance at the 50th anniversary celebration of the Japanese Fulbright Program which I had the privilege to attend myself.) Thus the Fulbright Fellowship I received opened many doors for me to pursue my research in Japan and helped me in arranging subsequent company visits for the study abroad programme. This was especially the case for access to the auto industry given that the particular Fulbright Fellowship I received was funded by a Japanese auto firm. Thus the first day I visited the sponsoring company I had the opportunity to meet with the CEO who indicated that he was very interested in seeing the results of my research and that I could have access to any information I needed to complete my work. In practice though, lower level managers were not always as forthcoming with the information I requested. Still, access to managers and data was much better than in the USA where I did not meet with anyone higher than plant manager and the corporate director of safety and health at either of the two US auto companies I visited.

I spent a great deal of time at this Japanese company and was even given a company uniform to wear during my all-day meetings. I also participated with members of the Safety and Health Department in morning exercises to the company song and in safety rituals (see photos). The only thing the CEO himself would not agree to was my request to work on the assembly line. He said I would probably hurt myself and mess up production. However, his executive assistant contacted other auto companies on my behalf to arrange visits for me—something that would be unheard of in the USA. As noted, prior to my Fulbright experience in Japan I had conducted research on OSH at US and European-owned auto firms' operations in the US, Europe, and one developing country (Kenya). Following my stay in Japan, I was able to use my Japanese contacts to arrange research visits to a number of Japanese auto plants in the USA. This allowed me to compare OSH and general CSR practices of a number of firms headquartered in the USA, Europe or Japan and operating in several countries (Wokutch, 1990a, 1992b).

Figure 1 Morning Safety Exercises at Host Firm

Source: Photos taken with author's camera by a Safety and Health Department staff member
at host firm.

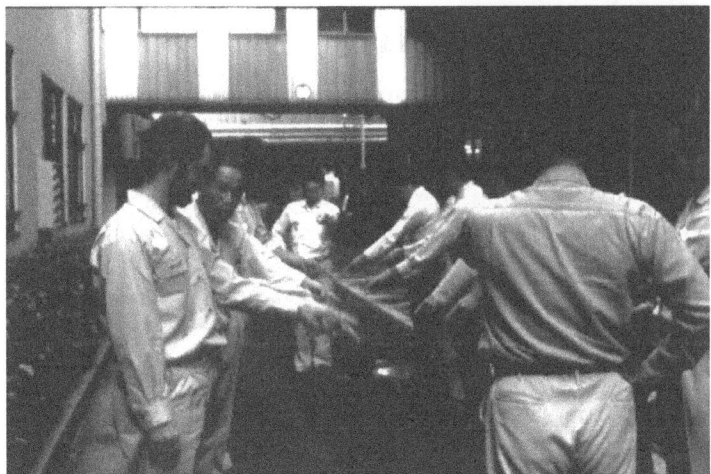

Research methods

The research methods employed in this research were multi-faceted. I conducted semi-structured interviews with OSH managers at most of the automotive plants I visited in Japan and the USA. In some cases I was also able to meet with plant or department managers, union officials and occasionally individual workers. I was also given access to very detailed company-and industry-level injury and illness statistics collected by the Japanese Automotive Manufacturers

Association. In addition, I made use of government statistics on OSH at the industry, private sector, and national levels. Along with interviewing industry representatives, I also spoke with government officials, union representatives, academicians, lawyers and labour rights activists concerned with OSH.

At the auto company funding my Fulbright Fellowship, my research approach contained elements of participant observation, despite my not being permitted to work on the assembly line. I spent several weeks at the main plant of this company conducting interviews and observing production. On a few occasions I was given the opportunity to roam around the production facilities as I pleased. Given that my height and weight were fairly typical for a Japanese worker, and given that I was dressed in a company uniform, it was easy for someone to mistake me for a typical worker from a distance. Thus I am quite confident that the observations I made about the nature of production and OSH activities when accompanied by OSH or production managers were typical of activities performed when no one in authority or a known visitor was watching. Moreover I was able to observe in training and also candidly talk with American workers, who were in Japan to learn the company's operating procedures and philosophy prior to the opening of a new production plant of this firm in the USA. Included among these were most of the safety and health staff. By very lucky coincidence, I had met with one of the senior US safety and health managers for this firm's new US plant in my earlier research when he was working for one of the 'big three' US auto companies and there was a level of trust already established. I was able to go out for dinner and drinks with him and the rest of the new American safety and health staff members in Japan for training and to get their very candid observations of the strengths and weaknesses of the Japanese approach to OSH relative to that of their former US employers. These candid observations in a casual environment made while these safety and health managers were just learning this new Japanese approach to safety and health management were invaluable in allowing me to differentiate between the Japanese managers' *tatemae* (party line or socially acceptable) statements about safety and health and the real or authentic state of affairs (*honne*).

The longitudinal nature of this study allows me to make some observations about the changing patterns of CSR practices over time. Over the years of conducting the OSH research and leading study abroad programmes to Japan I had the opportunity to meet with managers and/or staff from over 50 Japanese and American companies and other organisations operating in Japan. In addition, I had numerous casual encounters with Japanese, Americans and other individuals living in Japan as well as simple observations in daily life that helped me form the opinions expressed here.

Occupational safety and health

OSH is probably not one of the first issues one generally thinks of when discussing corporate social responsibility, but it actually is quite a useful issue to look at to consider a firm's overall approach to CSR. It is a corporate social performance dimension for which there is a great deal of logic for cooperation among labour, management, and government. Workers don't want to get injured or become sick; firms want to avoid injuries and illnesses which can be very costly in terms of lost production, healthcare expenses, retraining costs and other expenditures. Moreover national and regional OSH agencies have as their mission to improve safety and health conditions on the job, and serious workplace safety and health incidents can impose political costs to the party in power. Nevertheless, in the United States OSH has been both a political football and a matter of a great deal of contentiousness in labour–management relations (Wokutch, 1990a, b, 1992a). Probably nothing exemplifies this better than the infamous 'Cowboy *after* OSHA Inspection' cartoon (Western Training Company, n.d.) that shows a cowboy (an iconic symbol of free-spiritedness in the USA) riding a horse equipped with all sorts of safety devices including lights, training wheels, a net, and even a wagon behind the horse labelled as an 'emission control system'. So studying OSH in Japan, which is noted for a high level of cooperation among labour, management, and government, provided some particularly useful insights into differences in the nature of institutional relations in the two countries.

One of the things that first caught my attention when I started exploring worker safety and health in Japan is the graph of workplace injury and illness experience over time in the USA and Japan (Figure 1) which I have extended with more current data. This shows a Japanese injury and illness rate that is five times higher than that in the United States in 1952 declining to the point where they are equal in 1970 and further declining such that the rate is only one-quarter of that of the USA by 1985. (As shown in Figure 1, reported injury and illness rates in both countries have continued to decline since then.) The decline in these reported Japanese injury and illness rates is indeed very impressive, but there are both anecdotal and statistical reasons to be suspicious of the magnitude of the decline. During my interviews with Japanese workers, managers, OSH specialists and workers' advocates, there were frequent references to Japanese workers not reporting and, in fact, hiding injuries so as not to bring shame upon themselves and their work group and to help in achieving zero-accident goals set at the work group, factory, corporate, and even national levels. One Japanese OSH manager helping with the start-up of a US subsidiary of a Japanese auto firm even implied that Japanese workers were in some sense more honourable in hiding minor injuries compared with US workers who in his view ran to the medical station with every minor cut. Likewise, in the Japanese auto industry where the injury and illness statistics are collected on a firm-wide basis and there is a sense of competition among the firms in the industry, it is not uncommon to hear safety and health managers question the veracity of the injury and illness statistics of other firms.

Another reason for believing that there is substantial underreporting of injuries in Japan derives from a statistical relationship between major and minor injuries that safety and health pioneer Herbert Heinrich (1941) discovered almost a century ago. According to Heinrich, for every 300 accidents with no resulting injury there are 29 accidents with minor injuries and 1 with a major injury. Because the workplace injury and illness definitions in the United States and Japan are quite similar (Wokutch, 1992b, Wokutch and McLaughlin, 1988, 1992) there should be approximately equal ratios of total injuries and illnesses to worker fatalities in the two countries. But this is not the case by a long shot. For example for the period 1983–1987 there were 926 lost-work injuries and illnesses for every work fatality in the USA whereas the ratio was 142 to 1 in Japan. If Heinrich is to be believed, and almost a century worth of data supports his observation, then either the number of fatal injuries or the number of total injuries must be mistaken in the USA and/or Japan (Wokutch, 1992b, Wokutch and McLaughlin, 1992). It is possible that there could be some over-reporting of minor injuries and illnesses in the USA. Indeed there have been cases where individuals receiving workers compensation disability payments have their disability payments disallowed after being discovered engaging in other physically demanding activities such as the former New York firefighter who was discovered participating in kickboxing competitions (Seifman, 2011). But because companies and the government have motivations to catch cheaters it is easier to hide injuries or illnesses or not report them as work-related than it would be to feign non-existent ailments. Likewise it is vastly easier to hide a minor injury than it is to hide a fatality. Given that *overreporting* of non-fatal work-related injuries and illnesses and *underreporting* of work-related fatalities are likely to be relatively minimal in the USA, the logical conclusion is that *underreporting* of non-fatal injuries and illnesses in Japan is a far more likely reason for the disparity in the ratios reported above. This underreporting of non-fatal injuries and illnesses in Japan is also indicated by enormous differences in reported injury and illness rates between US and Japanese plants of the same Japanese auto companies (Wokutch, 1990b, 1992b).

The Japanese safety and health system

Although there are legitimate questions regarding the relative advantage of Japan versus the United States in terms of their overall safety and health performance it is still instructive to consider just how the Japanese have been able to reduce the rates of workplace injuries and illnesses so dramatically over time. I believe there are five key elements of the Japanese approach to OSH that have been responsible for this.

OSH management in harmony with productivity and quality management

In Japan, the management of OSH is considered to be highly congruent with the management of productivity and quality. There are several slogans conveying this relationship that are promoted by industry associations and governmental OSH agencies and that were prominently displayed at all the major firms I visited. Most notable of these are: *anzen daiichi* (safety first—a slogan most likely imported from abroad) and *anzen nakushite seisan nashi* (without safety there can be no production).

To fully understand the congruence between OSH and productivity and quality requires some explanation of the Japanese manufacturing system (also referred to as 'lean production'). Predominant characteristics of this system include small inventories of parts, team oriented production, a high degree of interdependence among workers within teams and between work groups, short production runs of different models of a given product (e.g. automobiles), rapid switching of the production line from model to model, and continuous improvement of efficiency and quality as preached through the production philosophy of *kaizen* (Imai, 1986; Ortiz, 2006; Schonberger, 1982). When you consider that the *kaizen* philosophy seeks to eliminate even the smallest defects and inefficiencies it is obvious that accidents, which are both a reflection of a major problem with the production process and a likely cause of further problems, should be avoided at all costs. Furthermore, the root causes of accidents that do occur must be discovered and eliminated immediately in order to get production back on line and to eliminate inefficiencies and defects in production.

OSH protections are integrated throughout the production system

According to the American OSH managers who had previously worked at US auto companies and at the time of this research were working with a Japanese auto firm in the USA, OSH concerns were more of an afterthought at their former US employers. In contrast with their Japanese employer OSH concerns were fundamental at the very earliest stages of the production planning process. In addition they noted that, with their Japanese employer, responsibility for maintaining a safe and healthy work environment is shared by workers, line managers and staff. This contrasted sharply with their descriptions of conditions at their former US employers where the OSH staff were viewed as having the primary responsibility for this. This view frequently resulted in disputes between OSH staff and line managers who were more concerned with production and quality.

Cooperative rather than punitive OSH regulatory approach

In research comparing the regulatory activities of the US Occupational Safety and Health Administration (OSHA) and its Japanese counterpart, the Labour Standards Bureau (Wokutch, 1992b), statistics on numbers and amounts of safety and health fines, percentage of inspections resulting in fines, and similar measures were examined. On all of the dimensions considered the Japanese exhibited a far less punitive and adversarial regulatory approach than exists in the USA.

OSH regulation in Japan is also less disturbed by partisan politics than in the United States. Evidence of this is in the far greater stability of staffing and budget levels in Japan relative to the United States. Moreover, we don't see the periodic cycles of tougher/more lax/then tougher – again enforcement when a major accident occurs as frequently happens in the USA (Wokutch, 1992b). There is, however, currently much more concern in Japan with enforcement of safety and health regulations in the aftermath of the Fukushima nuclear meltdown.

Behavioural rather than engineering orientation to OSH promotion

In Japan workers are trained in precise detail on the proper way to perform specific work routines so as to optimise productivity, quality and OSH. And, because Japanese workers are much more compliant with these directions than US workers, Japanese managers and government regulators can rely on individual workers to perform their jobs in exactly the prescribed manner.

Certainly the Japanese culture is one where deference to authority is much more ingrained than in the USA, but failure to comply with work rules can be punished severely in Japan. One anecdote is quite illustrative of this. A manager I interviewed who had originally insisted that all of his workers always follow all of the rules eventually conceded that there once was one worker who had annoyed him by ignoring several warnings about not wearing safety equipment. When he did this again, the manager sent the worker home early telling him he had forfeited the honour of being allowed to work that day. Moreover the next day when he came to work he was forced to wear a yellow shirt—a symbol of great disgrace—all day to identify him as someone who could or would not follow directions. OSH managers at this particular company where I heard this story were quite upset that the line manager had said anything about it and wanted to suppress the information. When asked why they were upset about this story, they indicated that being required to wear this yellow shirt was such a dishonour that the worker would have preferred to have been given the honour of committing suicide rather than bearing this shame! Needless to say, this sort of punishment sends a message to other workers and reinforces their compliance with work rules.

The fact that Japanese OSH managers and regulators can rely on workers to follow prescribed work routines is a great advantage. This behavioural orientation is far less expensive than the approach followed in the USA where we try to 'engineer' safety and health into the workplace. US OSH managers with whom I spoke in other phases of this research would frequently complain that machinery not only had to be 'foolproof' (safe enough to protect workers who make mistakes) but actually 'sabotage-proof' (containing mechanisms built in to stop workers from purposely overriding the safeguards preventing them from doing a job in a forbidden manner that the worker finds more convenient). Obviously this is quite costly.

Labour, management and government cooperation

The high level of cooperation among labour, management and government contrasts quite starkly with the situation in the USA where not only are safety and health issues matters of great controversy (recall the 'Cowboy *after* OSHA Inspection'), but even more problematically, OSH are sometimes used as proxy issues to gain negotiating leverage over other parties thereby undermining the legitimacy of OSH concerns (Wokutch 1990a, 1992b).

Weaknesses of the Japanese system

Although there is much to admire about the Japanese approach to the regulation and management of OSH in the workplace as indicated above, there are also several problems which I detail below.

Overly cooperative unions and regulators

There is a need for labour representatives and government regulators to fill an adversarial role and pose some threat to firms that neglect their OSH responsibilities. Because of the strong emphasis on cooperation neither unions nor regulators perform this function as effectively in Japan as in the USA, although the situation has improved since I first examined this issue. For example, in 1986 I heard stories of OSH managers taking government inspectors out for dinner and drinks in conjunction with inspection visits. According to a senior Japanese OSH official who I interviewed in 2011, that practice is no longer permitted.

Large versus small firm disparities

Because of the nature of the production system and the *kaizen* philosophy in Japan, large firms like the auto companies will exert constant pressure on their subcontractors to reduce costs and improve productivity and quality. They will often also subcontract out the most undesirable work—the so-called 'dirty, dangerous, and demanding' functions. Furthermore because of the relatively non-adversarial roles played by government regulators and labour there are much greater differences in the injury and illness rates of small versus large firms in Japan relative to those in the USA (Wokutch, 1990a, 1992a, b).

In-group versus out-of-group disparities

There are also great disparities on all sorts of dimensions regarding the treatment of 'insiders', permanent[2] workers, almost all of whom are Japanese males, versus those considered outsiders—temporary workers, foreigners,

---

2 This term is now somewhat anachronistic because of the increased occurrence of job changing in Japan in recent years.

ethnic minorities and in some sense even women who have traditionally been viewed as temporary workers (until marriage). There is evidence that this disparate treatment shows up in higher incidences of injuries at least for illegal immigrants (Yamagiwa, 1996).

Overemphasis on zero accidents

The emphasis on *zero* accidents can prove counterproductive in a culture such as Japan where the social pressures to conform are so strong that the saying 'the nail that sticks out gets hammered in' replaces the common US saying of 'the squeaky wheel gets the grease' in popular work culture. Thus, there is great unspoken pressure to hide injuries and illnesses unless there is no alternative. (Who would want to be the first worker to report an injury that would make the attainment of departmental, plant, company, indeed even national zero accident goals impossible?) The pressure to work through pain and discomfort is heightened by the nature of the lean production system with interdependent work teams and little slack. A worker is well aware that his or her co-workers will have to work extra hard if he or she has to miss work due to an injury or illness.

Operations in developing countries

In the 1980s there were stark contrasts between the great emphasis Japanese auto companies placed on transferring their OSH management system and culture to the new US plants that they were opening relative to the scarce attention given to this in plants they were opening at the same time in developing countries. A more recent visit to a Japanese auto plant operating in China suggests that the OSH practices there, at least now, are quite similar to those in Japanese plants in the USA and Japan. Given the history of conflict between China and Japan and the great market potential for the sale of autos in China, Japanese auto companies operating in that country would want to be very cautious of doing anything that might offend their Chinese hosts.

Karoshi[3]

This is the Japanese term for 'death from overwork' (Kanai, 2008; National Defense Counsel for Victims of Karoshi, 1990; Wokutch, 1994). Although *karoshi* is not a strictly Japanese phenomenon, this problem has received more attention in Japan and South Korea than in other countries, no doubt due to

---

3 This section of the paper dealing with *karoshi* benefited immensely from two interviews—25 years apart—and some email correspondence with Hiroshi Kawahito who is probably the leading expert in the world on this phenomenon. Kawahito is a lawyer who argued the first successful *karoshi* case before the Japanese Supreme Court and continues to represent clients in such cases. He is also a lecturer at the University of Tokyo. Unfortunately I did not record the exact dates of these interviews.

the excessively long working hours in those two countries and their cultural similarities. Even though we do not have a specific comparable English word for this phenomenon, we do talk about people 'working themselves to death'. The particular ways by which excessive work can lead to death are many and varied and occur to different degrees in different countries. Some examples of fatalities resulting from excessively long or hard work are heart attacks, strokes, fatal traffic accidents due to falling asleep at the wheel and even suicides. Such fatalities often occur when people are not technically 'on the job' but there can be questions about the work-relatedness of the fatalities. There are strong economic and psychological motivations for victims' families to have a death classified as work-related as *karoshi* is by definition. If the death is work-related the victim's family would be eligible for workers' compensation and they may also seek some admission of responsibility and an apology from the company for the death. Where the work-relatedness of a worker's death has not been acknowledged by the company, families have undertaken legal action to pursue their claims and Japanese courts have ruled in favour of victims' families in a number of such cases.

Implications for other dimensions of CSR in Japan

I believe that many of my findings with respect to the management of OSH apply to other aspects of CSR in Japan as well. In the USA a common view of CSR is that of balancing the interests of the various stakeholders of the firm with the intent of achieving some overall good. In Japan the interests of permanent employees and major shareholders are clearly favoured over those of other stakeholders. As noted, historically most permanent workers have been Japanese males. This results in a number of problems not only in the workplace but also in other domains of social activity in Japan for foreigners, racial and ethnic minorities, women and just about everyone outside of these permanent employees. Discrimination against these other groups of employees takes many forms. They will bear the brunt of changes in the need for labour, being hired and fired as needed, so that the benefits of the permanent employees can be maintained. As discussed above they also frequently get an inordinate amount of the dirty, dangerous, and demanding work piled on them. In the case of females, sexual harassment, though historically quite common in Japan, was not really widely recognised as a problem until the 1980s and the terminology for this phenomenon was even borrowed from English.

Other corporate stakeholders have also experienced surprisingly poor treatment by Japanese corporations over the years. Although customer service is exceptional in Japan, the prices consumers pay for products can be quite exorbitant. Discrimination, noted above with respect to employment, is also prominent towards consumers, especially foreigners. Even travel guides (travel.stackexchange.com, 2014) warn foreigners that discrimination based on appearance is entirely legal in Japan. The somewhat unpredictable treatment of foreigners contributes to the already significant public relations problem Japanese companies have in other parts of Asia stemming from lingering resentment dating back to World War II.

During the boom years of the Japanese economy, many individual shareholders invested in the Japanese stock market and made very substantial returns; however they have not fared so well in recent years. When the Japanese economic bubble burst in the late 1980s and early 1990s, the Japanese stock market collapsed and it has never fully recovered. The Nikkei average which hit a high of almost 40,000 at the end of 1989 is still at less than half that value. Moreover, stockholder influence and benefits are significantly diluted in Japan by the surprisingly strong influence that members of the Japanese mafia or yakuza wield over corporate affairs through threats and intimidation. Occasionally yakuza members are also employed by companies to keep dissident shareholders quiet.

As noted above, large corporations are able to use their market power to extract various sorts of advantages from their suppliers and subcontractors, leaving numerous problems for them to deal with. Also as noted above there are significant environmental problems in Japan. With its highly concentrated industry and high population density, environmental protection is challenging and the general public has suffered through significant environmental problems as the Japanese economy has grown (Hamilton and Kanabayashi, 1994). Two early environmental problems were Minamata disease resulting from the dumping of mercury wastes into Minamata Bay and Itai-Itai disease resulting from cadmium pollution (McKean, 1981). More recent and significant was the meltdown of reactors at the Fukushima nuclear power plant following the March 2011 earthquake and tsunami. Critics noted that there was very poor planning for this disaster as the back-up power generating system was located at the same place as the plant itself and was actually below sea level. The overwhelming public belief is that excessively cozy relationships among politicians, regulators and TEPCO management allowed this faulty planning to happen. Moreover, there is evidence that prudent safety measures were not undertaken out of concern they would alarm the public who were being told that nuclear power was safe (60 Minutes, 2014). Likewise, the public believes that overly zealous and loyal corporate employees withheld information and downplayed the dangers of the disaster in order to protect the corporate reputation.

In the period prior to the mid-1980s there was very little discussion of CSR in those terms. Nevertheless there was actually a good bit of social responsibility demonstrated by corporations, especially in terms of relations with their permanent workers. In one of the few early writings about CSR in Japan, Mafune (1988) noted that because Japanese corporations traditionally provided for many social welfare needs of their workers such as housing, hospitals, gyms, and even utilities and roads, there were relatively few occasions when the company needed to work with the local community. This could account for some of the negative views of CSR in Japan detailed here.

Motivations and determinants of CSR in Japan

In earlier work (Wokutch, 1990a, 1992b, Wokutch and Shepard, 1998), I suggested that there were three key determinants of CSR in Japan:

▶ **The within group–out of group distinction.** Those within the core of the Japanese corporate family such as permanent workers have been treated very well but this has led in many ways to discrimination of those outside this core group such as minorities, foreigners, and women

▶ **The sense of duty based on personal relationships arising from Confucianism.** When this relationship originated in feudal days commoners were bound by duty to their feudal lord who has been replaced by the feudal corporation which takes care of the permanent employee's every need and in return expects unquestioning loyalty

▶ **The sense of loyalty.** In the US the traditional hero archetype is the cowboy who is always striking out on his own, refusing to be tied down by obligations, whereas in Japan it is the samurai warrior who is loyal to the death. The Japanese samurai tradition of *bushido* also has a role to play in this. *Bushido* emphasises stoicism, loyalty, sacrifice, honour, and unquestioning obedience (Saito, 2008)

To the extent that loyalty between the employer and the employee is mutual this can produce some very positive benefits, helping companies and workers get through tough economic times. It can also promote ethical conduct within the company without having to resort to complex and detailed codes of conduct. There can however be serious negative ramifications as well such as in Toshiba's sale of classified defence technology to the former Soviet Union, the widespread sale of HIV-tainted blood, and the Daiwa bond trading scandal (Hamilton, 1996; Hamilton and Kanabayashi, 1994; WuDunn, 1997; Feldman, 1997; Rosenblatt, 1987). In such cases employees have put the interests of the company ahead of the interests of society.

Pressures forcing changes upon Japan

Both the understanding and practice of CSR in Japan have changed dramatically for the better since I first started studying this topic. Back in 1986 when I first began this research it was hard to find anyone in Japan who was familiar with the term 'corporate social responsibility'. Research in the field—at least using this terminology—was limited, with the exception of Mafune's (1988) early contributions. Now the use of the term CSR is as common in Japanese corporate circles as it is in the USA and there are very sophisticated/slick looking CSR reports on the websites of most large Japanese companies. There also seems to have been a great increase in Japanese companies having formal CSR departments. In addition, CSR and business ethics have become popular academic subjects in Japan and there are quite a few active researchers in this field, with many of these researchers belonging to the Japan Association of Business Ethics Scholars. There is also considerable evidence that not only have the communications, language, and corporate structures pertaining to CSR changed in Japan, but so too has the performance associated with carrying out CSR policies, and for the better. (A fuller discussion of the evolution of the thinking and practice pertaining to CSR in Japan is contained in Wokutch and Shepard, 1999.)

I believe that the greater internationalisation of Japanese society has had a very large role to play in these changes. As corporate managers have been dispatched and lived overseas, they and their family members have brought back with them many perspectives and values that are working their way through Japanese society. Certainly things like greater equality for women, interest in activities other than school for children, and greater individual freedom in general are aspects of life in the USA to which many Japanese dispatched there grow accustomed.

Likewise the influx of foreigners into Japan has also brought about changes. This influx has been hastened by the low birth rate and the ageing of Japanese society, resulting in more job openings than native Japanese can fill, although, like in the USA, many of the jobs foreigners fill are undesirable ones. The low birth rate itself can be attributed to the fact that there have been significant improvements in the opportunities for women over the course of my research and many young women are choosing to postpone marriage as they don't want to get trapped in the housewife roles they have seen their mothers and grandmothers experience.

The presence of large multinational companies in Japan has also been a catalyst for change in the thinking and practice regarding CSR. Because women have historically been treated so poorly by Japanese companies, US and European companies operating in Japan have been very appealing employers for Japanese women and these MNCs have had a built-in advantage in attracting some of the best talent in Japan. Thus Japanese companies have had to become more progressive in their treatment of women out of sheer self-interest, whether they consider it a matter of CSR or not.

No doubt one of the greatest and long-lasting influences on CSR thinking and practice in Japan has been the events of 3/11 and their aftermath. Although the earthquake and tsunami could not be blamed on anyone, the meltdown of the Fukushima nuclear reactors has been widely blamed on lack of preparedness of the Tokyo Electric Power Company (TEPCO). Government regulators were viewed as complicit in their lack of oversight and unwillingness to force TEPCO to do serious emergency preparedness planning prior to 3/11 for fear that this would be unsettling to the Japanese people who were already sceptical of the safety of nuclear power on which Japan relied heavily. Likewise the overwhelming public belief is that overly zealous and loyal corporate employees withheld information and played down the negative effects of the disaster in order to protect its corporate reputation (Singal et al., forthcoming).

Despite this lack of preparedness on the part of the company, many TEPCO workers demonstrated outstanding bravery and a sense of duty/loyalty both to the company and to their country in combating the disaster. More than 4,000 TEPCO workers continue to brave the high levels of radiation in their efforts to clean up the site, a task that is expected to take approximately 30–40 years (60 Minutes, 2014).

The bravery of the TEPCO Fukushima workers has been inspiring, and so too has been the response of Japanese companies to help out in the crisis. The responses of the Japanese people, as well as non-Japanese MNCs operating in Japan, have also been inspiring. Many companies, both Japanese and MNCs, provided help using their core competencies in a manner consistent with the notion of strategic CSR (Porter and Kramer, 2006). In 2011 interviews with executives in the Nissan Public Relations Department these officials noted that they contacted suppliers and other members of their extended corporate family in the Fukushima area immediately after the disaster to find out what they could do to help. They were informed that, with the shutdown of the Fukushima facility, a lack of power was a serious problem. They quickly realised that their Nissan Leaf hybrid vehicle could serve as a mobile generator and they dispatched 50 of these vehicles to the Fukushima region. Toyota followed a similar strategy of assistance.

Omron, a Japanese company that specialises in sensing and monitoring technology, checked with their people in the region and found out that a number of hospitals in the region were destroyed by the tsunami and those that remained were overcrowded and in need of additional equipment and supplies. After checking with the hospital staff, they dispatched volunteer Omron employees to the area to deliver equipment that would allow the medical personnel operating there to treat these patients better. Two devices that were particularly useful were nebulisers because of the crowded conditions and risk of the spread of infectious diseases and battery powered health monitoring devices such as those used to measure blood pressure because of the lack of electricity in the region. They also provided the region with traffic signals and automatic teller machines to replace those that had been destroyed on 3/11. According to Omron officials a total of approximately 1,000 field engineers equipped with Geiger counters were sent to the stricken region to assist in the recovery efforts (Omron, 2011).

On the American side, FedEx utilised its core competence of quick transport and delivery of packages to get relief supplies to the affected area and Walmart rapidly donated and delivered relief supplies to the stricken area. Other American firms followed similar strategies of help consistent with their core competencies.

Such activities noted above show an inherent understanding of the principles of strategic CSR but certain collective activities show a distinctive Japanese spin to CSR that I think is very encouraging for the future. In the aftermath of the 3/11 disaster, there has been a severe power shortage in Japan since all of the country's nuclear power plants with the Fukushima Daiichi design were shut down for precautionary reasons. In response to this the entire auto industry moved their 'weekend' to Thursday and Friday and worked on Saturday and Sunday to help even out the demand for power. Likewise there have been national 'Cool Biz' and 'Super Cool Biz' campaigns to get industry to conserve power during Japan's sweltering summers by raising the thermostat at workplaces. The normally very formal Japanese workers were encouraged to come to work in short-sleeved shirts and leave their more formal attire at home. Citizens were also asked to voluntarily conserve energy at home. These campaigns produced even more energy savings than targeted (Onishi with Suzuki, 2011). Thinking back to the violence at gas stations in the USA during the 1973 and 1979 oil shortages, it seems that the solidarity of the Japanese people has some built-in advantages in terms of managing CSR. Although the Japanese traditions of isolation and insularity have some profoundly negative implications for CSR, the ability to pull together in the face of disaster is indeed impressive and encouraging for Japan as it faces future challenges.

References

60 Minutes. (2014). Fukushima: Three Years Later. www.cbsnews.com/videos/fukushima-three-years-later/. Aired April 16.

Feldman, E. A. (1997). 'Deconstructing the Japanese HIV Scandal'. JPRI Working Paper No. 30, Japan Policy Research Group: February.

Fucini, J. L. and S. Fucini. (1990). *Working for the Japanese: Inside America's Mazda Plant.* Free Press: New York.

Hamilton, D. P. (1996). 'Blood Pact: In Japan AIDS Scandal, Many Wonder if Safety Came Second to Trade'. *Wall Street Journal.* October, 9: A1, A6.

Hamilton, D. P. and M. Kanabayashi. (1994). 'Belief Grows that Japan's Environment Has Been Sacrificed for the Economy'. *Wall Street Journal.* May, 13: A

Heinrich, H. W. (1941). *Industrial Accident Prevention: A Scientific Approach.* McGraw-Hill: New York.

Imai, M. (1986). *Kaizen: The Key to Japan's Competitive Success.* Random House: New York.

Japan Institute of Labour. (1988). *Industrial Safety and Health.* Industrial Relations Series 9. Tokyo.

Kamata, S. (1982). *Japan in the Passing Lane.* Translated and edited by Tatsuru Akimoto. Pantheon: New York.

Kanai, A. (2009). 'Karoshi (Work to Death) in Japan'. *Journal of Business Ethics,* 209-216.

Kazuo, K. (1991). *The Economics of Work in Japan.* Toyo Keizai Inc.: Tokyo.

Mafune, Y. (1988). 'Corporate Social Performance and Policy in Japan'. In *Research in Corporate Social Performance and Policy,* L. E. Preston (Ed.). JAI Press: Greenwich, Conn., pp. 291-303.

National Defense Counsel for Victims of Karoshi. (1990). *Karoshi: When the 'Corporate Warrior' Dies.* Mado-Sha: Tokyo.

National Safety Council (2010). *Injury Facts, 2010 Edition.* Itasca, IL.

Omron. Disaster Response Report. (2011). Available: www.omron.com/ir/irlib/pdfs/m · 11 e/arl l 24e.pdf, accessed: 11/7/11.

Onishi, N. with K. Suzuki. (2011). 'Japanese, in Shortage, Willingly Ration Watts' *New York Times,* On-line Asia Pacific edition, July 29, 2011, accessed 11/5/11. Available: www .nvtimes.com/201 J /07/29/world/asia/29electricit y .html ?pagewanted =all

Ortiz, C. A. (2006). *Kaizen Assembly: Designing, Constructing, and Managing a Lean Assembly Line*. CRC Taylor & Francis: Boca Raton, FL.

Ouchi, W. (1981). *Theory Z: How Americans Can Meet the Japanese Challenge*. Addison-Wesley: Reading, Mass.

Pascale, R. and A. Athos. (1981). *The Art of Japanese Management: Applications for American Executives*. Warner Books: New York.

Porter, M. and M. R. Kramer. (2006). 'Strategy & Society: The Link between Competitive Advantage and Corporate Social Responsibility'. *Harvard Business Review*. December, pp. 1-14.

Rosenblatt, R. A. (1987). 'Toshiba Sale "Criminal", Japanese Says'. *Los Angeles Times* July 18. Available: http://articles.latimes.com/1987-07-18/news/mn-736_1_japanese-government Accessed 4/13/2014.

Saito, A. (2008). 'Bushido' *Encyclopedia of Business Ethics and Society*, R. Kolb, Ed., Vol. 1, pp. 208-210, Thousand Oaks, CA: Sage.

Schonberger, R. (1982). *Japanese Manufacturing Techniques*. Free Press: New York.

Seifman, D. (2011). 'City "Disables" Pension' *New York Post*. Available: http://nypost .com/2011/05/22/city-disables-pension/ Accessed 4/13/14.

Sethi, S. P., N. Namiki, and C. Swanson. (1984). *The False Promise of Japanese Management*. Pitman: Boston.

Singal, M., R. E. Wokutch, Y. Poria, and M. Hong. (forthcoming). 'Ethical Decision-making in Extreme Operating Environments: Kew Garden Principles and Strategic CSR in Three Scenarios'. *Journal of Business and Professional Ethics*.

Travel Stack Exchange (2014). 'Can I Side-Step Discrimination Against Foreigners in Japan?' Available: http://travel.stackexchange.com/questions/4978/can-i-side-step-discrimination-against-foreigners-in-japan accessed 4/6/14.

Western Training Company (N.D.). 'The Cowboy *after* OSHA Inspection'. Available: http://community.ubnt.com/t5/The-Lounge/The-Cowboy-After-OSHA/td-p/395890. Accessed 7/18/14.

Wokutch, R. E. (1990a). *Cooperation and Conflict in Occupational Safety and Health: A Multination Study in the Automotive Industry*. New York: Praeger.

Wokutch, R. E. (1990b). 'Corporate Social Responsibility Japanese Style'. *Academy of Management Executive*, 4: 56-74.

Wokutch, R. E. (1992a). 'Myths of the Japanese Factory'. *Journal of Commerce*, August 26: 10A.

Wokutch, R. E. (1992b). *Worker Protection, Japanese Style: Occupational Safety and Health in the Auto Industry*. Ithaca, NY: ILR Press, Cornell University.

Wokutch, R. E. (1994). 'Special Report: Work: Dying for It in Japan'. In *Medical and Health Annual, Encyclopedia Britannica*, pp. 373-375.

Wokutch, R. E. and J. McLaughlin. (1988). 'The Socio-Political Context of Occupational Injuries'. In Preston, L.E. (ed.) *Research on Corporate Social Performance and Policy*, 10, pp. 113-137.

Wokutch, R. E. and J. McLaughlin (1992). 'The US and Japanese Work Injury and Illness Experience'. *Monthly Labor Review*. April: 3-11.

Wokutch, R. E. and Shepard, J. M. (1999). 'Corporate Social Responsibility Implications of the Maturing of the Japanese Economy'. *Business Ethics Quarterly*, Vol. 9, No. 3, pp. 527-540.

WuDunn, S. (1997). 'Daiwa Bond Trader Puts His Spin on Scandal'. *New York Times*. January 13, Available: www.nytimes.com/1997/01/13/business/daiwa-bond-trader-puts-his-spin-on-scandal.html Accessed: July 18. 2014.

Yamagiwa, H. (1996). 'Accidents Add to Illegals' Plight'. *The Japan Times*. June 14: p. 3.

Figure 1 US and Japanese injury and illness experience, 1952–2008

Data drawn from: United States 1952–1988 from Japan Institute of Labour, 1988; United States 1988–2008 from National Safety Council, 2010; Japan from Japan Institute of Labour, 1988 and personal correspondence.

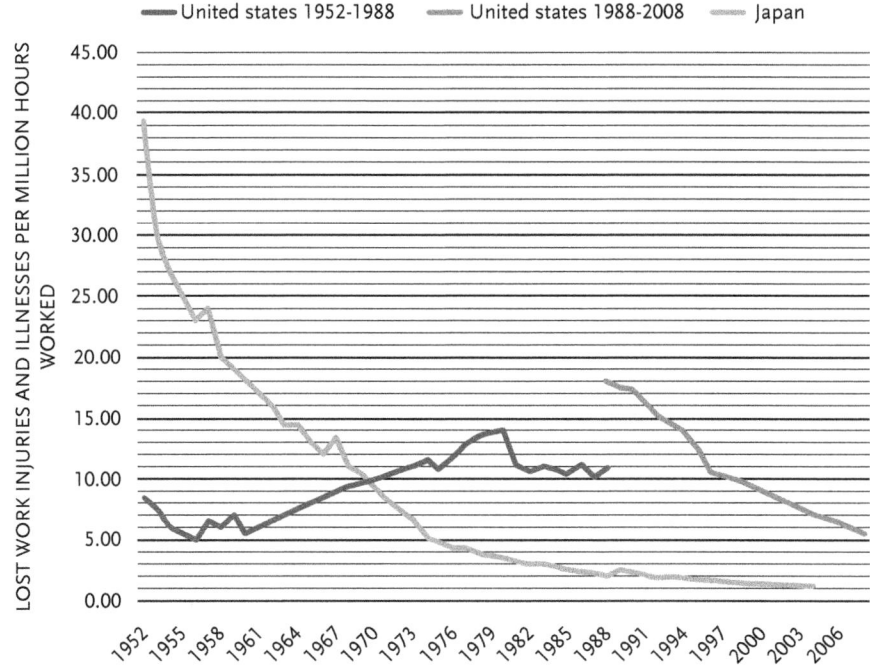

The Journal of Corporate Citizenship Issue 56 *December 2014* © Greenleaf Publishing 2014

DOI: [10.9774/GLEAF.8757.2014.de.00003]

Financial Materiality of Sustainability

The Japanese Context

Patrick Albrecht
PricewaterhouseCoopers Sustainability Co., Ltd, Japan

Christopher Greenwald
RobecoSAM AG, Switzerland

This paper examines Japanese companies in the context of an emerging focus on the financial materiality of sustainability. Specifically, we address the question of how many Japanese companies identify and quantify financial benefits of their sustainability initiatives in their public reporting compared with international peers. Drawing upon original data from the 2013 Dow Jones Sustainability Index (DJSI) assessment, we demonstrate that Japanese companies out-perform other geographies on reporting the business benefits of their environmental initiatives while under-performing in reporting a similar link on social aspects as well as linking sustainability to the broader corporate strategy. We analyse the reporting of business benefits in the environmental domain of 14 Japanese companies from the automotive and technology industries. For this we focus on their reporting against the Japanese Environmental Accounting Guidelines, which we identified as a key reason behind the detailed reporting on business benefits. We conclude by recommending Japanese companies to improve their reporting on financial materiality by extending beyond the current focus on environmental conservation to the full range of environmental and social issues as well as by including indirect benefits in their assessment and reporting of benefits.

- Strategic sustainability management
- Responsible investment
- Environmental accounting
- Sustainability valuation

Patrick Albrecht is Manager at PricewaterhouseCoopers Sustainability Co., Ltd in Tokyo, consulting multinational companies based in Japan on sustainability strategy, management and reporting. He is particularly interested in the interaction of Japanese companies with the international investment community around ESG issues. Before moving to Japan in 2012 he supported PwC Germany's Sustainability team since 2008. Prior to joining PwC Germany, he was research assistant and completed his PhD at the Centre for Sustainability Management (CSM) and the Institute for Environmental and Sustainability Communication (INFU) of Leuphana University Lueneburg.

✉ PricewaterhouseCoopers Aarata, PricewaterhouseCoopers Sustainability Co., Ltd, Sumitomo Fudosan Shiodome Hamarikyu Bldg., 8-21-1 Ginza, Chuo-ku, Tokyo 104-0061, Japan

📞 +81 (0)80 4466 1919

💻 patrick.p.albrecht@jp.pwc.com

Christopher Greenwald is Head of Sustainability Investing Research at RobecoSAM and oversees RobecoSAM's research related to the Dow Jones Sustainability Index. Prior to joining RobecoSAM, Christopher was Director of ESG Data Content for ASSET4/Thomson Reuters where he was head of the research department and responsible for the integration strategy of ESG content at Thomson Reuters. Christopher holds an MBA from HEC Lausanne as well as a Certificate in Financial Asset Management Engineering from the Swiss Finance Institute. He also holds a PhD in political science from Duke University and has previously taught at the University of Chicago.

✉ RobecoSAM AG, Josefstrasse 218, CH-8005 Zürich, Switzerland

📞 +41 44 653 12 59

💻 christopher.greenwald@robecosam.com

N THE PAST SEVERAL YEARS, the leading companies in sustainability have become increasingly focused on developing a more sophisticated understanding of the positive business and financial benefits of their sustainability initiatives. This paper examines Japanese companies in the context of this emerging focus on the financial materiality of sustainability. Drawing upon original data from the 2013 Dow Jones Sustainability Index (DJSI) assessment of RobecoSAM, we demonstrate that Japanese companies out-perform other geographies on reporting the business benefits of their environmental initiatives while under-performing in reporting a similar link on social aspects as well as linking sustainability to the broader corporate strategy. In the second part of the paper, we analyse the reporting of a small sample of Japanese companies on the business benefits of their environmental initiatives. We base this analysis on the Japanese Environmental Accounting Guidelines which appear to be a major driver behind the widespread reporting of monetary benefits related to environmental initiatives. Finally, we provide two recommendations for how Japanese companies can improve their reporting on financial materiality, drawing specifically on Michael Porter's conception of **creating shared value**. In addition to providing original results on Japanese sustainability reporting, we believe that this study can help companies link their sustainability disclosures with their business benefits, thereby improving the material relevance of their sustainability reporting.

Starting point: sustainability initiatives add value

The past several years have seen a rise in interest in **integrated reporting**, which encourages companies to focus their reporting to their capital providers on the value creation for the organisation and for others over time (IIRC 2013). This requires 'businesses to make clearer links between financial and non-financial key performance indicators (KPIs)' (Blacksun 2012). Within this context, it is important to understand how Japanese companies report on the material importance of their sustainability initiatives as well as how they might be able to improve. To frame this discussion, we begin by outlining recent considerations that encourage companies to more directly link their sustainability initiatives with financial and material importance.

Investors are interested in understanding individual value drivers and risks for a broad range of issues, beyond the current Japanese focus on environmental conservation. According to a 2012 survey by SustainAbility in partnership with Bloomberg of over 1,000 investment professionals, about 80% of investors consider ESG (environmental, social and governance) aspects at least sometimes. Governance aspects, in particular ethics and board independence are most often considered. Social aspects (customer relationship management and health & safety top that list) follow, before environmental aspects of which energy efficiency is the top concern (SustainAbility 2012). Companies and investors today largely agree that

> ESG factors can have long-term consequences on a company's financial perform-
> ance, either for better or for worse. They accept that ESG factors are now at the core
> of business. However, the depth and breadth of ESG factors are not fully valued by
> investors and company management (WBCSD and UNEP FI 2010: 7).

One of the key barriers is in measuring and communicating the value contribution of sustainability. Both corporate executives and investors base their decisions on comparable, financial information about the costs and benefits of certain scenarios (UN Global Compact LEAD; UN PRI 2013). A clearer and more sophisticated link between sustainability and business impacts is therefore essential in order for sustainability to be mainstreamed into the core strategic decision making processes of both companies and investors.

While the quest for a business case for corporate social responsibility has been pursued in the research literature since the 1980s, recently Michael Porter and Mark Kramer have introduced the concept of creating shared value (CSV) which may be helpful in allowing companies to re-formulate their sustainability initiatives as more central to their business strategy. Porter and Kramer's idea places value creation at the centre, and emphasises the need for companies to focus their sustainability initiatives on those areas where there is a substantial benefit for the business and society (Porter and Kramer 2006, 2011). While it can be argued that they contrasted their approach with a very narrow definition of CSR (corporate social responsibility) that did not reflect the actual status of CSR at the time (Beschorner 2013; Crane *et al.* 2014), their approach has notably changed the attitude of many business executives and contributed to a more strategic understanding of sustainability initiatives and will probably lead to real improvements in business practice (Dyllick 2014).

The Japanese context

Previous studies on CSR in Japanese companies show very widespread adoption of CSR practices at least since the early 2000s. In a study of the online reporting of the top 50 Japanese companies, Fukukawa and Moon (2003) found 90% to be claiming to report on CSR. In particular, environmental reporting experienced a dramatic increase from the 11% found in a previous study by Yamagami and Kokubu (1991) to 90.2% in 2002 (Fukukawa and Moon 2003). Japanese companies are similarly active as European companies and significantly more so than US companies (see e.g. Kolk 2008).

Yet, a sceptical attitude towards CSR becomes evident, as a recent survey of global executives demonstrated (Accenture 2012; *based on responses from 250 executives globally, 40 of which from Japan*): globally, 83% of senior decision makers view spending on sustainability initiatives as investment rather than costs. In Japan, however, only 42% view spending on sustainability initiatives as investment. With 58% the majority of Japanese executives view sustainability initiatives instead rather as costs.

Making the business case for sustainability initiatives and demonstrating how the company creates shared value requires quantifying how sustainability adds value, which in turn allows sustainability to be understood as not simply a cost of doing business but rather as an investment with clearly defined benefits.

Against this backdrop we want to extend the research focus on Japanese companies to a key element of the CSV concept: the identification of business benefits related to their sustainability initiatives. More specifically we address the question of how many Japanese companies identify and quantify financial benefits of their sustainability initiatives in their public reporting compared with international peers.

We address this question first by examining empirical data on the reporting of the business benefits of sustainability in Japan and globally from the 2013 DJSI assessment, before then analysing the context of Japanese sustainability reporting and in particular the Japanese Environmental Accounting Guidelines.

Financial materiality aspects in the DJSI assessment

To better understand how Japanese companies link sustainability initiatives to business value compared with the rest of the world, we examine data from the 2013 DJSI assessment.[1] In particular, we focus on two questions in the DJSI assessment on the financial materiality of environmental and social issues in companies' annual or sustainability reporting. These two questions consider whether companies provide a discussion in their sustainability reporting that balances the needs of various stakeholders in relation to the business interests of the company. The most common approach companies employ for this in their reporting is through a 'materiality matrix' where the most important issues for stakeholders are plotted against the issues that are most important for the business. In addition, the two questions ask companies whether they provide

---

1 All of the data in this section represents original data from the 2013 Dow Jones Sustainability Index (DJSI) Corporate Sustainability Assessment conducted annually by RobecoSAM. The sample includes 185 Japanese companies compared with an overall universe size of 1,834 companies globally. The data is derived through a combination of direct company inputs via an online questionnaire supplemented by an analysis of corporate public disclosures. This data sample was chosen given the relevance of the assessment's reporting questions for measuring the material link between companies' corporate sustainability disclosures.

clear examples in their reporting of sustainability initiatives that led to either cost savings or revenue generation. The questions ask for such business impact examples both for environmental initiatives and social initiatives. In addition, the questions examine whether the examples provided are anecdotal or strategic in nature (i.e. applying across the entire company) and whether the company can provide some quantification of the cost savings or revenue generation. The rationale behind both of the questions is that in order for mainstream investors to integrate sustainability into their financial evaluations of companies, it is increasingly important for companies to demonstrate a clear link in financial terms between their sustainability investments on the one hand and their business value on the other.

Japanese companies lead in linking environmental initiatives and business value

Most notably and perhaps surprisingly from the results of the data, Japanese companies actually lead all other regions in the world in linking environmental initiatives to their economic impacts in their sustainability reporting. The majority of Japanese companies (55.7%) provide some link in their reporting between environmental initiatives and cost savings, and this is clearly higher than the global average of 45.7%, and notably higher than the average for Asia of 32.1% (see Fig. 1).

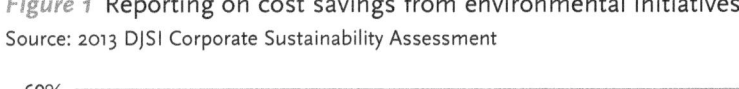

Figure 1 Reporting on cost savings from environmental initiatives
Source: 2013 DJSI Corporate Sustainability Assessment

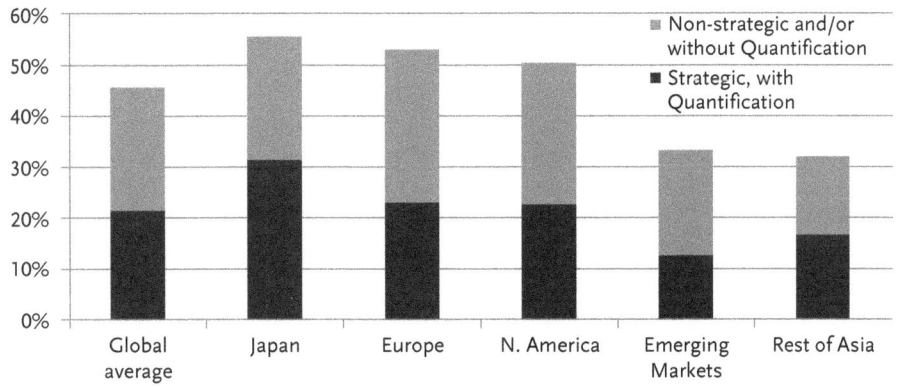

Not only are Japanese companies ahead in reporting a link with cost savings, but they also much more frequently provide examples in their reporting that are strategic (i.e. company-wide) and with a quantification of the benefits; 31.4% of Japanese companies provide a strategic and quantified link with cost savings vs. a 21.4% average for companies globally.

In addition to leading the rest of the world on reporting a link between environmental initiatives and cost savings, Japanese companies also demonstrate leadership in reporting examples of revenue opportunities linked to initiatives, products or services which have a positive environmental impact. Japanese companies provide examples of revenue generation in 39.4% of the cases, compared with only 23.4% for companies globally and 16.6% for companies in the rest of Asia (Fig. 2). Thus, Japanese companies provide more examples than other companies throughout the world of ways in which they can derive both cost saving as well as revenue opportunities from their environmental initiatives and products.

Figure 2 Reporting on revenue generation from environmental initiatives
Source: 2013 DJSI Corporate Sustainability Assessment

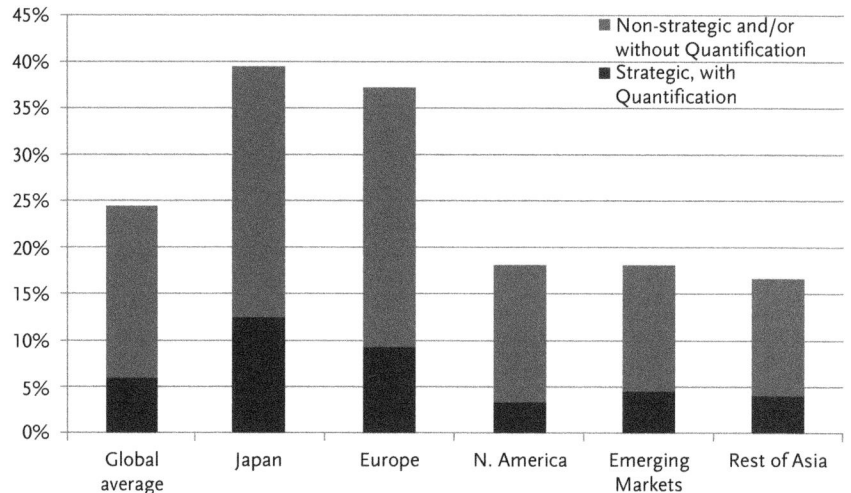

Japanese companies lag in linking social initiative and business value

In contrast to the leading position of Japanese companies on linking environmental initiatives to their business impacts, Japanese companies were relatively weak in making similar links for social initiatives. Only 1.1% of Japanese companies provide a link between social initiatives and cost savings vs. 7.6% of companies globally (Fig. 3). Moreover, there are no Japanese companies in the entire set of companies assessed that provide a strategically significant example of cost savings with quantification of impact.

Figure 3 Reporting on social cost savings

Source: 2013 DJSI Corporate Sustainability Assessment

Reporting on Social Cost Savings	Global average	Japan	Europe	N. America	Emerging Markets	Rest of Asia
Strategic with Quantification	2.2%	0.0%	3.9%	1.6%	2.6%	2.0%
Non-strategic and/or without Quantification	5.4%	1.1%	9.3%	5.0%	2.3%	5.9%
Total	7.6%	1.1%	13.2%	6.6%	4.9%	7.9%

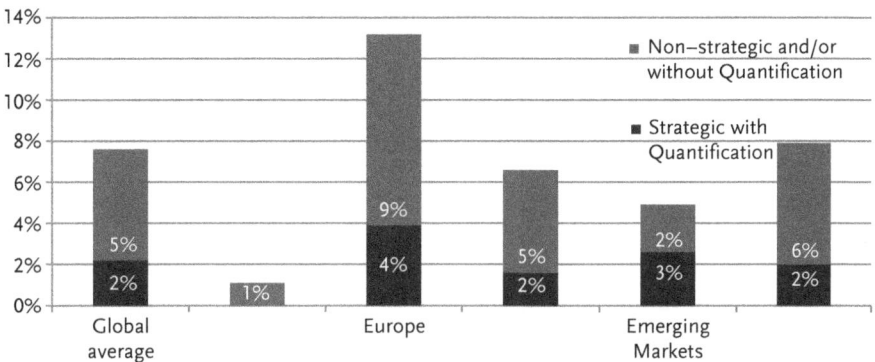

While companies find reporting a link between sustainability initiatives and cost savings challenging throughout the world, this challenge is particularly significant for Japanese companies. Although this failure to link social initiatives with cost savings represents a clear weakness for Japanese firms, it also represents an opportunity for Japanese companies to improve their reporting in this area. Programmes targeted at improving employee engagement and productivity have significant economic benefits across many industries, and explaining these links would help investors make better sense of the value-added from companies' investments in social programmes.

In reporting on revenue opportunities from social programmes, Japanese companies were in line with the global average, with 10.8% of Japanese companies providing such a link (Fig. 4). However, Japanese companies were below average in providing strategic examples with a quantification of impacts, with only 0.5% of Japanese companies providing this in their reporting.

Figure 4 Reporting on revenue generation from social initiatives

Source: 2013 DJSI Corporate Sustainability Assessment

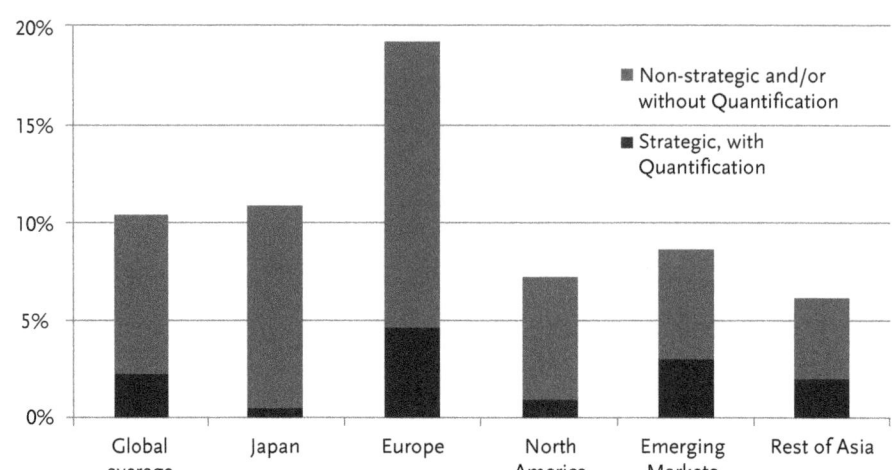

While reporting on this link is also challenging for companies globally, with only 2.2% of companies providing strategic examples with a quantitative impact, Japanese companies clearly also have an opportunity to clarify the link between social programmes, products or services and their positive economic benefit.

Japanese companies also lag on disclosing a materiality framework

In addition to being challenged in linking social initiatives to their economic benefits, Japanese companies are also below average in providing an overall explanation of a tool or framework whereby they balance sustainability initiatives with their business impacts. Japanese companies disclosed such a framework, usually in the form of a 'materiality matrix' 18.9% of the time vs. the global average of 29.4% (Fig. 5). On this factor, European companies demonstrate clear leadership, with 45.8% of the companies providing a materiality matrix and/or a discussion of the framework to balance the interests of stakeholders with the business interest of the company.

Figure 5 Reporting on materiality framework
Source: 2013 DJSI Corporate Sustainability Assessment

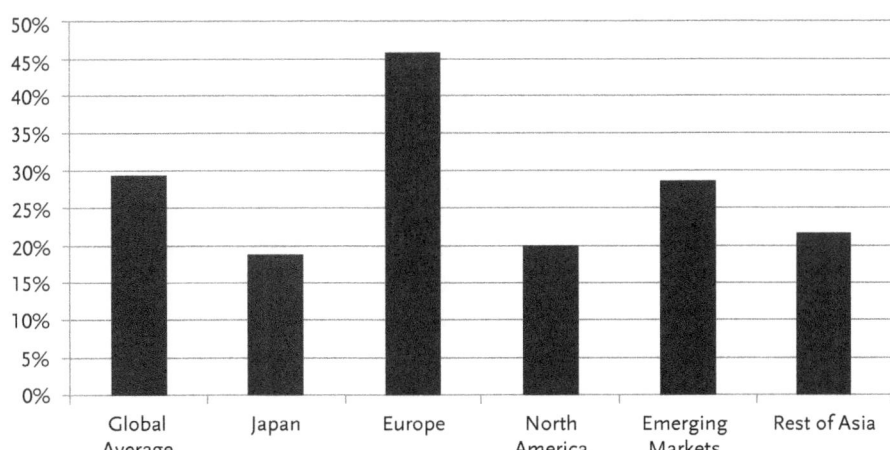

The result on the reporting of a materiality framework suggests that while Japanese companies provide good examples on the link between environmental initiatives and their business impacts, they often lack an overall strategic orientation of these examples, around a more general strategic alignment between their sustainability strategy and the business goals of the company as a whole. Japanese companies clearly have a solid and indeed leading basis for providing these links, especially for environmental issues, but they could increase the relevance of their reporting by placing their reported examples of environmental cost and revenue benefits in the overall context of the business strategy of the company.

Why do many Japanese companies report links of environmental aspects and financial benefits?

Our analysis based on the DJSI assessment showed that more Japanese companies link environmental initiatives to revenue generation and cost savings in their public reporting compared with their international peers.

As the DJSI assessment introduced questions on this topic only recently in 2012, data on when this comparatively extensive reporting was established is not available from that source. Previous studies, however, indicate that this is a long-standing development. Saka and Burritt (2003) observed a rapid growth of both environmental reporting and environmental accounting for the period between 1998 and 2002.

They point to government initiatives as the 'first and main driver of environmental reporting and environmental accounting disclosures' and in particular to the Japan Ministry of Environment (MoE)'s Environmental Accounting Guidelines as the main driver for disclosure on environmental accounting, which includes requirements to report on revenue generation and cost savings achieved by environmental initiatives.

The MoE guidelines distinguish the practice in Japan from Europe and the US as they focus on external disclosure rather than internal management (see e.g. Kokubu and Kurasaka 2002; Nashioka 2003; Kokubu and Nashioka 2009). Nashioka (2003) found that 78% of companies that disclose environmental accounting use the MOE guidelines when they establish their environmental accounting system. Therefore, widespread application of the Environmental Accounting Guidelines appears to be a key reason for the relatively high level of reporting on financial benefits by Japanese companies. Therefore, we further investigate the application of the guidelines for public reporting. We do not further investigate the link between the reporting based on these guidelines and management practices (see e.g. Kokubu and Nashioka 2009), alternative government initiatives more targeted at internal management practices (namely the Environmental Management Accounting and Material flow cost accounting promoted by METI, see e.g. METI 2002, 2007, 2011; Onishi *et al.* 2008; Wagner *et al.* 2010) or other approaches developed individually by the reporting companies.

The Environmental Accounting Guidelines

The Japan Ministry of Environment (MoE) first introduced the Environmental Accounting Guidelines in 2000, and then updated them in 2002 and 2005. The guidelines aim to:

> allow a company to identify the cost of environmental conservation during the normal course of business, identify benefit gained from such activities, provide the best possible means of quantitative measurement (in monetary value or physical units) and support the communication of its results (MoE 2005: 3).

Thus companies are asked to identify costs and benefits from environmental conservation, defined as 'prevention, reduction, and/or avoidance of environmental impact, removal of such impact, restoration following the occurrence of a disaster, and other activities'. Based on the MoE's annual 'Survey of Environmental Friendly Corporate Activities' of about 3,000 of the largest companies in Japan, 730 had introduced environmental accounting following their guidelines by 2010. This rate of more than 25% of companies applying the guidelines is remarkable, making the country certainly one of the global leaders in this practice. Yet, as Figure 6 shows, the use of the guidelines appears to have stagnated since 2006, and is about at the same level in 2010 as it was in 2004, which may point to some limitations or frustrations on the side of applying companies.

Figure 6 Status of applying the Environmental Accounting Guidelines

Note: Based on data from MoE (2013)

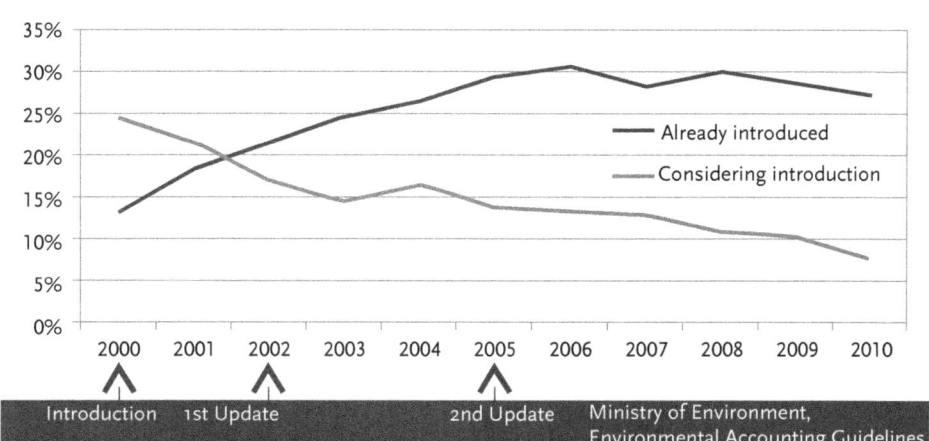

How do companies use the Environmental Accounting Guidelines?

To understand more about the benefits and potential limitations of the guidelines, we went on to investigate the reporting against the guidelines. Large multinational companies are commonly most advanced in their reporting practices as they face most investor interest and commonly have sufficient internal capacities to respond to these demands. To select companies for a sample, we therefore first limited our selection to the largest Japanese companies based on the 2013 Fortune Global 500 ranking, a ranking of the largest 500 corporations worldwide by revenue (resulting in 62 Japanese companies in 2013). We further limited our selection to industries that were most strongly represented in the top 100 of this list with three companies each (see Table 1): 'Motor vehicles' as well as 'Electronics, electrical equipment'. We then extended the sample by industries adjacent to the electronics, electrical equipment industry, namely 'Computers, office equipment' and 'Information technology services', covering Japanese technology companies as an industry group. We therefore focus broadly on two industries: Japanese car makers and technology companies, resulting in a small sample of five car makers and nine technology companies. Due to this small sample size, we do not aim at an empirical assessment of the guidelines, but rather at qualitatively identifying the nature of the reported information as well as identifying good practices.

Table 1 Japanese companies in Top 100 of the Fortune Global 500 list

Note: basis for selection of industry focus for analysis of individual reports. Most frequent industries highlighted in bold font

Fortune Global 500 rank	Company	Industry
8	Toyota Motor	**Motor vehicles**
13	Japan Post Holdings	Insurance: life, health
32	Nippon Telegraph & Telephone	Telecommunications
44	JX Holdings	Petroleum refining
45	Honda Motor	**Motor vehicles**
47	Nissan Motor	**Motor vehicles**
54	Hitachi	**Electronics, electrical equipment**
83	Panasonic	**Electronics, electrical equipment**
86	Nippon Life Insurance	Insurance: life, health
94	Sony	**Electronics, electrical equipment**

All companies selected (see Appendix) report the costs and/or investments of their environmental initiatives, and with the exception of Sony all of them also report the benefits, either cumulative or broken down by cost savings and revenue generation in more detail, confirming our finding from the DJSI assessment that Japanese companies widely report on cost savings and revenue generation for environmental initiatives. In addition to the availability of data on cost savings and revenue generation, a compelling business case for sustainability initiatives would require that the reported data demonstrates a positive net benefit of the spending for sustainability initiatives. To get an understanding of the relationship between reported spending and benefits, we normalised the reported data on costs and investments as well as revenues and cost savings as percentage of total revenue in the reporting period.

Figure 7 shows that Japanese car makers primarily report costs. In all other categories the reported numbers seem insignificant compared with these costs. With a broader definition, both investments and benefits should feature more significantly in the reporting. For example, German car maker Volkswagen announced in March 2012 that more than two-thirds of its €62.4 billion investment programme for the next five years will be directly or indirectly spent on 'ever more efficient vehicles, powertrains and technologies, as well as environmentally compatible production'. With total revenues of €197 billion in 2013, a roughly estimated €8.3 billion annual investment in environmental technologies would result in a ratio of 4.2% of revenue (Volkswagen 2012).

Figure 7 Environmental accounting data – Global 500 Japanese car makers

Note: Information on environmental accounting based on latest available sustainability, CSR or environmental report as of 31 July 2013. Company selection and normalisation based on total revenues from Fortune Global 500 list 2013 converted with JPY94.215 for US$1, exchange rate as of 31 March 2013, end of the Japanese financial year 2013

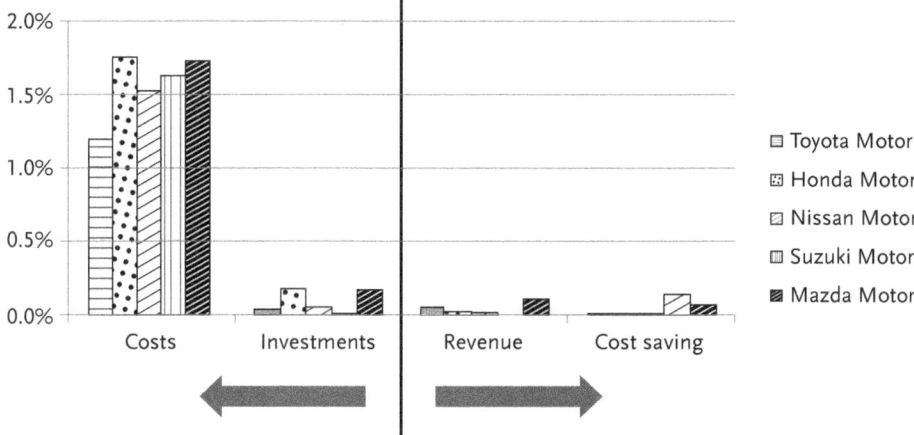

Looking at the same data for selected technology companies, Figure 8 shows a different picture. First, all companies summarised revenue generation and cost saving into a single benefits category. More importantly, two of the analysed companies, Fujitsu and Toshiba, report significant benefits, exceeding the reported costs.

Figure 8 Environmental accounting data – Global 500 Japanese technology companies

Note: Information on environmental accounting based on latest available sustainability, CSR or environmental report as of 20 January 2014. Company selection and normalisation based on total revenues from Fortune Global 500 list 2013 converted with JPY94.215 for US$1, exchange rate as of 31 March 2013, end of the Japanese financial year 2013

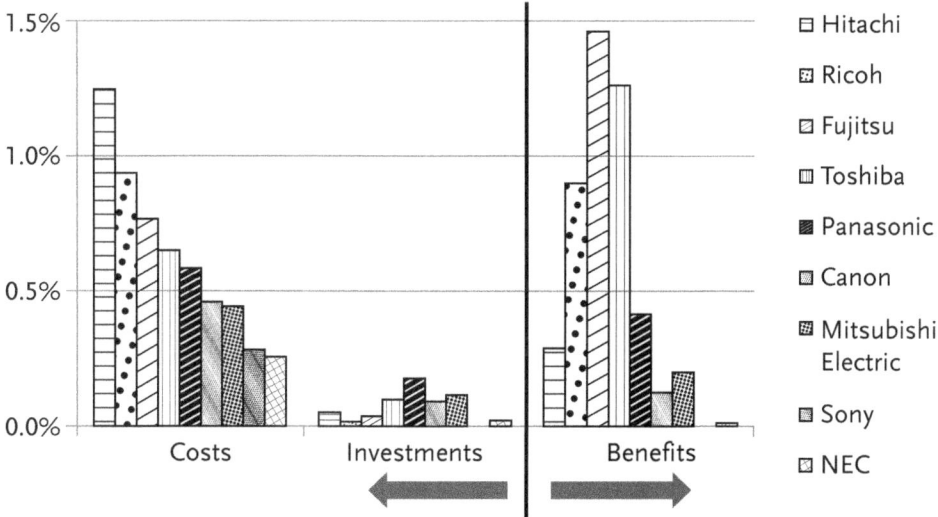

Both companies that report significant benefits of their environmental activities—Fujitsu and Toshiba—include estimated benefits (see Fig. 9 for Fujitsu). In addition, for example, Fujitsu describes its accounting methodologies and underlying assumptions in considerable detail and interprets the results from the perspective of the company, adding an element of narrative reporting and linkage to corporate strategy that is often missing in Japanese company's reporting against the guidelines.

Figure 9 Fujitsu's reporting on environmental costs and benefits
Source: Fujitsu Group (2013)

Trends in Costs and Economic Benefits

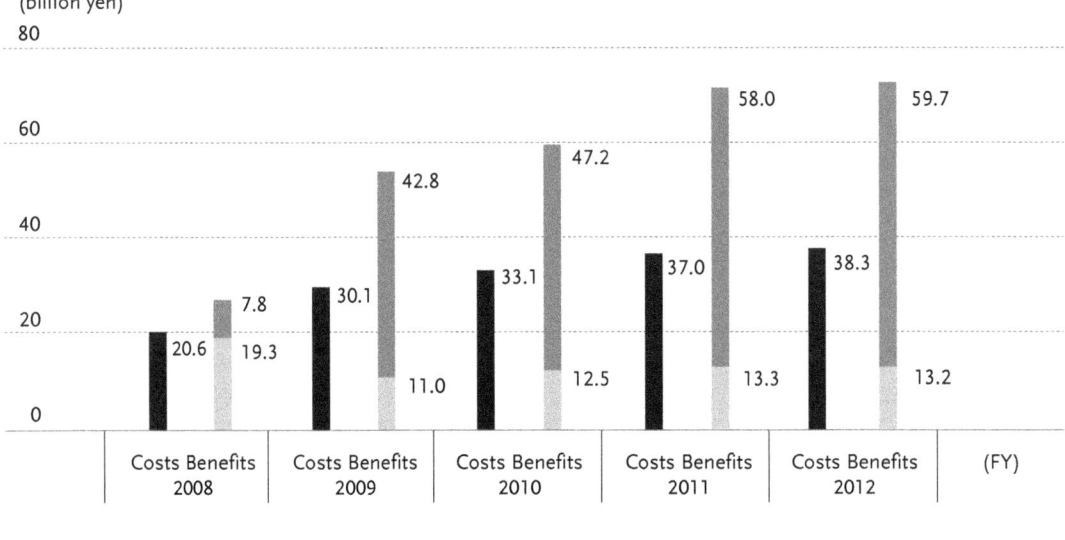

We therefore conclude our brief investigation into the Japanese Environmental Accounting Guidelines with the following observations:

▶ A large number of Japanese companies apply the guidelines

▶ Following the guidelines, the focus is on environmental conservation activities, not including environmental products or broader sustainability (e.g. social aspects)

▶ Reporting companies collect some data on revenues and costs savings; however, due to a focus on 'actual', proven benefits, overall the reporting of costs dominates

▶ A few selected companies such as Fujitsu take a broader approach by including 'estimated benefits' in their reporting. This allows them to make a more compelling case for their spending on environmental conservation

Need for a broader framework for managing and measuring value

We can conclude our analysis with two main conclusions and two recommendations for how Japanese companies can improve.

Conclusion 1. Looking at the results of the DJSI assessment, we can see that Japanese companies are leading globally in providing examples of both the cost savings and revenue benefits of their environmental initiatives. Nonetheless, Japanese companies are weaker than other companies globally in providing these links with regard to social initiatives and in providing a broader context of the relation between their sustainability strategy and their overall corporate strategy.

Conclusion 2. The MoE Guidelines for Environmental Accounting are the most likely key driver for the strong reporting on cost savings and revenue benefits examples of the Japanese companies in the environmental domain. The Japanese context provides a valuable example for the rest of the world of the successful mainstreaming of environmental accounting practices.

Looking at a small sample of company reporting, we could see that in practice mostly costs are reported. This imbalance can be attributed to the general design of the MoE guidelines and may be an expression of the historical tendency of many Japanese companies to be reactive to regulation. Several good practice examples, however, demonstrate that going beyond the minimum requirements prescribed by guidelines such as the MoE guidelines may allow companies to present a more compelling business case for environmental initiatives, and thus make reporting more relevant for investors and other stakeholders.

It appears particularly important to include indirect, estimated benefits into the equation, more than is currently done in the Guidelines for Environmental Accounting.

In order for Japanese companies to further develop their strengths and to address their relative weakness, we provide two recommendations:

Recommendation 1. Extend the assessment of financial benefits from environmental conservation to the full range of environmental and social issues.

If, as outlined in the CSV concept, sustainability is to move into the core of the business, the identification of business benefits cannot be limited to environmental conservation. For the most material issues, value drivers should be identified and impacts measured and reported. Standards or comprehensive guidelines on how to go about undertaking such a comprehensive valuation are yet to emerge. However, some companies, e.g. SAP as part of its integrated reporting journey, are taking first steps to more thoroughly understand and report the impact of social, environmental and other non-financial aspects on the company's business success (see Fig. 10).

Figure 10 Example of sustainability aspects impacting revenue at SAP
Source: SAP Integrated Report 2013

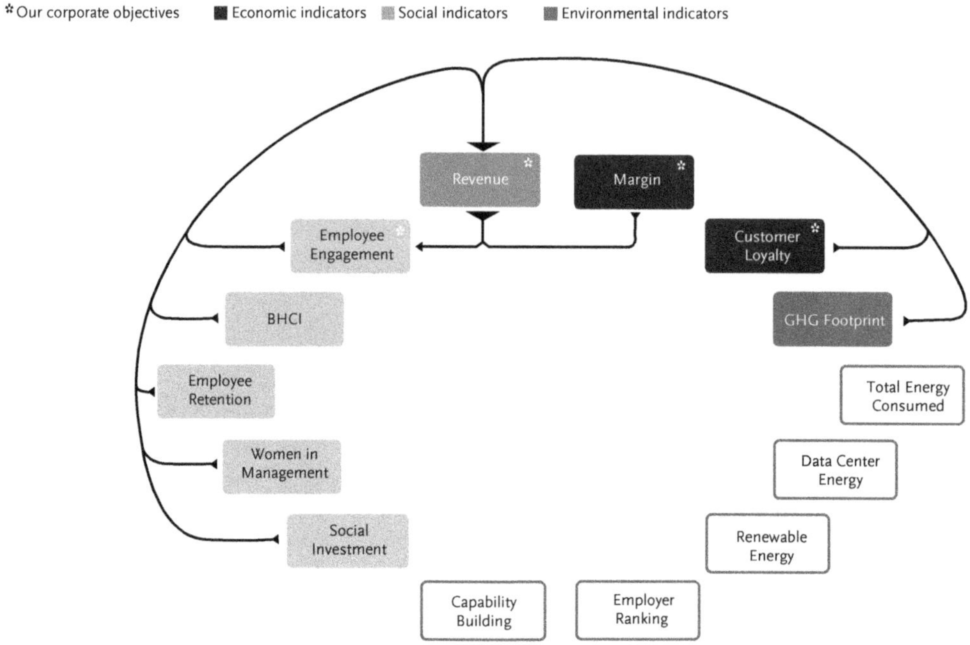

✿ Our corporate objectives ■ Economic indicators ▦ Social indicators ■ Environmental indicators

The strong experience of Japanese companies in environmental accounting should place them in a good position to move to a more comprehensive analysis of the impacts of sustainability on their businesses.

Recommendation 2. Japanese companies should further develop their accounting of all financially material aspects in decision making, including both direct and indirect benefits, and report these results to investors.

Investors appear to acknowledge that the shareholder value of sustainability is real. However, it always includes indirect value that is difficult to monetise such as improved customer relationships, better reputation, etc. If a company can determine that its sustainability initiatives actually bring benefits that exceed their costs, sustainability may become more central to its business strategy as outlined in the CSV concept.

In recent years sustainability valuation approaches have been developed and advanced that can be applied to quantify both direct and indirect value to enable companies to monetise, prioritise and communicate the shareholder value of sustainability. Risks and uncertainties of value components are recognised and valued (Kieffel 2012).

Recognising all factors can transform decisions: only looking at direct cost savings and revenue increases, projected financials may display a mediocre return on investment (ROI) for the initiative. Expanding the ROI framework to include the indirect benefits, the ROI often becomes a lot more compelling (see Fig. 11).

Figure 11 More compelling ROI through integration of indirect benefits

Source: based on PwC (2012)

Note: please note that this is an illustrative example unrelated to the above case study

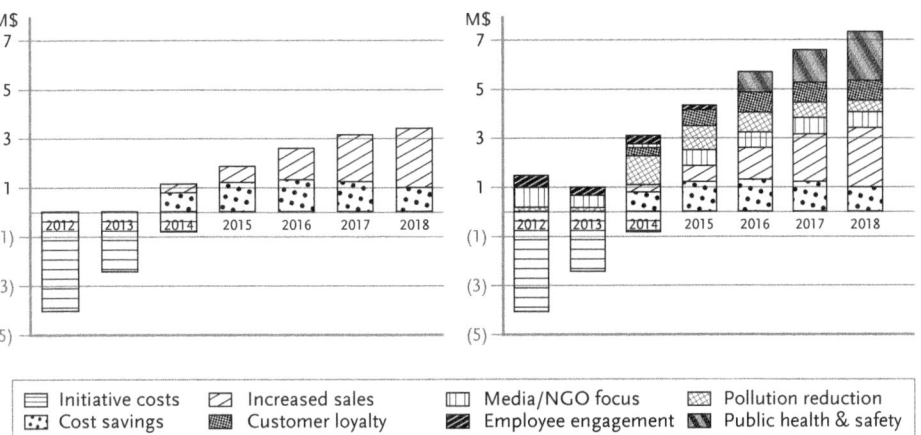

▤ Initiative costs	▨ Increased sales	▥ Media/NGO focus	▧ Pollution reduction
⁘ Cost savings	▦ Customer loyalty	▰ Employee engagement	◣ Public health & safety

Embracing a broader framework by asking what aspects matter for the project and company success as well as embracing uncertainty of future and often indirect benefits is challenging, and as we could see from the sample of reporting against the MoE Environmental Accounting Guidelines many Japanese companies prefer to stay with the hard proven 'actual' benefits. But it may well be necessary to succeed in the long term by avoiding short-sighted decisions and to identify sustainability investments for which scaling up makes sound business sense. Building on their long-standing experience with environmental accounting, we believe Japanese companies are well-equipped to integrate non-financials more broadly into their decision making processes. The full picture is needed to identify the sustainability initiatives that deliver value both for the company and society—and to apply them at scale. Possibly this would lead Japanese executives to see a greater opportunity in sustainability rather than primarily its costs.

Appendix: Environmental accounting information reported by selected companies

General company information		Revenue		Environmental accounting information										Source
Company	Industry (based on Global Fortune 500)	US$, billion	JPY, billion	Costs		Investments		Revenue		Cost savings		Overall benefit		(web page or page Sustainability/Environmental Report)
				JPY, billion	% of revenue	JPY, billion	% of revenue	JPY, billion	% of revenue	JPY, billion	% of revenue	JPY, billion	% of revenue	
Toyota Motor	Motor vehicles	266	25,033	299.5	1.2%	8.9	0.0%	13.9	0.06%	1.3	0.01%	15.2	0.06%	http://www.toyota-global.com/sustainability/environmental_responsibility/data/data30.html
Honda Motor	Motor vehicles	119	11,212	196.3	1.8%	19.56	0.2%	2.4	0.02%	0.3	0.00%	2.7	0.02%	Environmental Annual Report 2013, p.59
Nissan Motor	Motor vehicles	116	10,929	166.0	1.5%	5.52	0.1%	1.704	0.02%	0.9	0.01%	2.604	0.02%	Sustainability Report 2013, p.130
Suzuki Motor	Motor vehicles	31	2,921	47.6	1.6%	0.25	0.0%	0	0.00%	4.04	0.14%	4.04	0.14%	Environmental & Social Report 2013, p.26

Mazda Motor	Motor vehicles	27	2,497	43.1	1.7%	4.147	0.2%	2.717	0.11%	1.666	0.07%	4.383	0.18%	http://www.mazda.com/csr/environment/management/accounting.html
Fujitsu	Computers, office equipment	53	4,975	38.3	0.8%	1.99	0.0%					72.89	1.47%	http://www.fujitsu.com/global/about/environment/management/accounting/account2012/
Canon	Computers, office equipment	44	4,108	19.1	0.5%	3.81	0.1%	1.65	0.04%	3.47	0.08%	5.12	0.12%	http://www.canon.com/environment/management/accounting.html
Ricoh	Computers, office equipment	23	2,167	20.5	0.9%	0.39	0.0%	17.72	0.82%	1.84	0.08%	19.56	0.90%	https://www.ricoh.com/environment/account/index2012.html
Hitachi	Electronics, electrical equipment	109	10,260	127.9	1.2%	5.28	0.1%					29.92	0.29%	http://www.hitachi.com/environment/activities/stakeholder_collabo/account.html

General company information				Environmental accounting information											Source
Company	Industry (based on Global Fortune 500)	Revenue		Costs		Investments		Revenue		Cost savings		Overall benefit			(web page or page Sustainability/Environmental Report)
		US$, billion	JPY, billion	JPY, billion	% of revenue	JPY, billion	% of revenue	JPY, billion	% of revenue	JPY, billion	% of revenue	JPY, billion	% of revenue		
Panasonic	Electronics, electrical equipment	88	8,281	48.3	0.6%	14.94	0.2%					34.161	0.41%		Eco ideas Report 2012, p.38
Sony	Electronics, electrical equipment	82	7,716	22.1	0.3%										http://www.sony.net/SonyInfo/csr_report/environment/data/cost/index.html
Toshiba	Electronics, electrical equipment	70	6,576	43.1	0.7%	6.523	0.1%					83.175	1.26%		Environmental Report 2013, p.59/60
Mitsubishi Electric	Electronics, electrical equipment	43	4,051	18.1	0.4%	4.68	0.1%	4.27	0.11%	4.01	0.10%	8.28	0.20%		http://www.mitsubishielectric.com/company/environment/report/data/accounting/index.html
NEC	Information technology services	37	3,486	9.0	0.3%	0.752	0.0%					0.482	0.01%		http://www.nec.com/en/global/eco/announce/accounting/

Note: Information on environmental accounting based on latest available sustainability, CSR or environmental report as of 20 January 2014. Company selection and normalisation based on total revenues from Fortune Global 500 list 2013 converted with JPY94.215 for US$1, exchange rate as of 31 March 2013, end of the Japanese financial year 2013

References

Accenture (2012): *Long-Term Growth, Short-Term Differentiation and Profits from Sustainable Products and Services. A global survey of business executives* [Online] Available from http://www.accenture.com/SiteCollectionDocuments/PDF/Accenture-Long-Term-Growth-Short-Term-Differentiation-and-Profits-from-Sustainable-Products-and-Services.pdf [Accessed: November 14, 2013]

Beschorner, T. (2013): 'Creating Shared Value: The One-Trick Pony Approach'. *Business Ethics Journal Review* 1(17): 106–112.

BlackSun Plc (2012): Understanding transformation: Building the business case for integrated reporting. [Online] Available from http://www.blacksunplc.com/corporate/iirc_understanding_transformation/projet/BUILDING-THE-BUSINESS-CASE-FOR-INTEGRATED-REPORTING.pdf [Accessed: February 10, 2013]

Carroll, A. and Shabana, K. (2010): The business case for corporate social responsibility. A review of concepts, research and practice. *International Journal of Management Reviews*, 12(1), 85–105.

Crane, A., Palazzo, G., Spence, L.J., Matten, D. (2014): Contesting the Value of 'Creating Shared Value. *California Management Review*, Vol. 56, No. 2, pp. 130–153

Dyllick, T. (2014): The opposing perspectives on creating shared value. Financial Times.com, 24 April 2014 [Online] Available from http://www.ft.com/intl/cms/s/2/88013970-b34d-11e3-b09d-00144feabdc0.html#axzz38N5apl3Y [Accessed: January 10, 2014]

Figge F., Hahn, T., Schaltegger, S., Wagner, M. (2002): The Sustainability Balanced Scorecard: Linking Sustainability Management to Business Strategy. *Business Strategy and the Environment*, 11, p. 269–284.

Fujitsu Group (2013): FY 2012 Environmental Accounting Results. [Online] Available from http://www.fujitsu.com/global/about/environment/management/accounting/account2012/ [Accessed: January 10, 2014]

Fukukawa, K. and Moon, J. (2003): A Japanese model of corporate social responsibility: A study of website reporting. *Journal of Corporate Citizenship*, 16, 45-59.

Fukukawa, K. and Teramoto, Y. (2009): Understanding Japanese CSR: The reflections of managers in the field of global operations. *Journal of Business Ethics*, 85(1), 133-146.

IIRC (2013): The International <IR> Framework. [Online] Available from http://www.theiirc.org/wp-content/uploads/2013/12/13-12-08-THE-INTERNATIONAL-IR-FRAMEWORK-2-1.pdf [Accessed: January 7, 2014]

Japan. Ministry of Economy, Trade and Industry METI (2002): *Environmental Management Accounting (EMA) Workbook 2002* [Online] Available from http://www.meti.go.jp/policy/eco_business/pdf/workbook.pdf. [Accessed: December 10, 2013]

Japan. Ministry of Economy, Trade and Industry METI (2007), *Guidelines for Material Flow Cost Accounting (Ver.1)*. [Online] Available from http://www.meti.go.jp/policy/eco_business/pdf/mfca%20guide20070822.pdf [Accessed: December 10, 2013]

Japan. Ministry of Economy, Trade and Industry METI (2011), *Material Flow Cost Accounting: MFCA case example 2011*. [Online] Available from http://www.jmac.co.jp/mfca/thinking/data/MFCA_Case_example_e2011.pdf [Accessed: December 10, 2013]

Japan. Ministry of the Environment MoE (2005): Environmental Accounting Guidelines 2005. [Online] Available from http://www.env.go.jp/en/policy/ssee/eag05.pdf [Accessed: August 20, 2013]

Japan. Ministry of the Environment MoE (2013): *Annual Report on Environmental Statistics 2012*. [Online] Available from: http://www.env.go.jp/en/statistics/. [Accessed: August 20, 2013]

Kieffel, H.C. (2012): *Sustainability valuation: An oxymoron?* PwC US [Online] http://www .pwc.com/en_US/us/transaction-services/publications/assets/pwc-sustainability-valua tion.pdf [Accessed: August 5, 2013]

Kokubu and Kurasaka (2002): Corporate Environmental Accounting: A Japanese Perspective. In M. Bennett, J. Bouma and T. Wolters (eds.), *Environmental Management Accounting*, Kluwer Academic Publishers, p.161-173.

Kokubu and Nashioka (2009): Environmental Management Accounting Practices in Japanese Manufacturing Sites. *Environmental Management Accounting for Cleaner Production Eco-Efficiency in Industry and Science*, Volume 24, 2008, p. 365-376

Kolk, A. (2003): Trends in sustainability reporting by the Fortune Global 250. *Business Strategy and the Environment* 12(5): 279-291

Kolk, A. (2008): Sustainability, accountability and corporate governance: exploring multinationals' reporting practices. *Business Strategy and the Environment* 17 (1), pp. 1-15.

Nashioka, E. (2003): Current Status and Issues of Environmental Accounting Disclosure of Japanese Corporation. In Kokubu, K. and Eliko N. (eds). *Environmental Accounting in the process of updating*, p.175-196. (in Japanese)

OECD (2010), *Measuring Innovation: A New Perspective*, OECD Publishing, Paris.

Onishi, Y., Kokubu, K. and Nakajima, M. (2008): Implementing Material Flow Cost Accounting. In S. Schaltegger, M. Bennett, R. Burritt and C. Jasch (eds.), *Environmental Management Accounting for Cleaner Production*, Springer: Dordrecht, p. 395-409.

Porter, M. and Kramer, M, (2006): Strategy & Society: The Link between Competitive Advantage and Corporate Social Responsibility. *Harvard Business Review*, December 2006.

Porter, M and Kramer, M. (2011), Creating Shared Value, *Harvard Business Review* 89(1/2). p. 62–77.

Saka, C. and Burritt, R.L. (2003), Environmental accounting in Japan – recent evidence, *Journal of Asia-Pacific Centre for Environmental Accountability*, 9(4): 4-9.

SAP (2014): SAP Integrated Report 2013. Strategy and Business Model. Integrated Performance Analysis [Online] http://www.sapintegratedreport.com/2013/en/strategy-and-busi ness-model/integrated-performance-analysis.html [Accessed: June 8, 2014]

SustainAbility (2012): Rate the Raters. Phase Five. The Investor View. November 2012 [Online] http://www.sustainability.com/library/rate-the-raters-phase-five-1 [Accessed: July 2, 2013]

UN Global Compact LEAD and UN PRI (2013): *Enhancing company-investor communication* [Online]. January 2013. Available from: http://www.unglobalcompact.org/docs/ issues_doc/lead/Enhancing_Compacy_Investor_Communication_ESG_IB_Project.pdf [Accessed: January 10 2014].

UNEP FI and WBCSD (2010): *Translating ESG into sustainable business value* [Online] March 2010. Available from: http://www.unepfi.org/fileadmin/documents/translatingESG.pdf [Accessed: March 28 2014].

Wokutch, R. (1990): Corporate Social Responsibility Japanese Style. *The Executive*. 4 (2), 56-74.

Yamagami, T. and Kokubu, K. (1991): A Note on Corporate Social Disclosure in Japan, *Accounting Auditing & Accountability Journal*, 4 (4), pp.32-39.

DOI: [10.9774/GLEAF.8757.2014.de.00004]

CSR, Biodiversity and Japan's Stakeholder Approach to the Global Bumble Bee Trade[*]

Carol Reade
San José State University, USA

Koichi Goka
National Institute for Environmental Studies, Japan

Robbin Thorp
University of California, Davis, USA

Masahiro Mitsuhata
Arysta LifeScience, Japan

Marius Wasbauer
University of California, Davis, USA

Corporate social responsibility (CSR) embodies corporate concern for the natural environment. Biodiversity, however, is a relatively unfamiliar concept in the corporate lexicon, and comparatively little attention has been given to the effects of business on biodiversity and ecosystem health despite their fundamental role in human well-being. Adopting an interdisciplinary lens, we draw on the management, sustainability, and entomology literature to examine biodiversity as a CSR challenge highlighting the commercial bumble bee trade. We propose that Japan is emerging as a role model on the global stage as illustrated by its stakeholder approach to balancing commercial interests and ecological concerns associated with the global bumble bee trade. We conclude with implications for CSR.

- CSR
- Biodiversity
- Global bumble bee trade
- Invasive species
- Japan

* We thank Akira Shimizu for igniting the spark that led to this paper, and colleagues at the Association of Japanese Business Studies and anonymous reviewers for valuable comments on earlier drafts. Support from a San José State University Lucas College and Graduate School of Business Research Grant is gratefully acknowledged.

Carol Reade is associate professor of international management, San José State University. She is also a regular visiting faculty at Sophia University in Tokyo, where she teaches Japanese Business and Management. Her research focuses on the interface between the global firm and the external environment. Areas of interest include culture, indigenous knowledge, societal conflict and employee behaviour, and stakeholder relations. She has participated in entomological field expeditions and has been honoured with two new species named for her.

✉ Associate Professor, School of Global Innovation and Leadership, Lucas College and Graduate School of Business, San José State University, One Washington Square, San José, CA 95192-0164, USA

☎ +1-408-924-1343

📠 +1-408-924-6885

🖥 carol.reade@sjsu.edu

Koichi Goka is professor, Invasive Alien Species Research Team, National Institute for Environmental Studies, Japan. His research includes ecological risk assessment of invasive alien species, and the effects of pesticides on biodiversity. He is actively involved in the development of methods and systems for controlling invasive species, and has published extensively in scientific journals on invasive bumble bees in Japan.

✉ Invasive Alien Species Research Team, National Institute for Environmental Studies, Japan 16-2, Onogawa, Tsukuba, Ibaraki 305-8506, Japan

☎ +81-029-850-2480

📠 +81-029-850-2582

🖥 goka@nies.go.jp

Robbin Thorp is professor emeritus of entomology at University of California, Davis. A world authority on bumble bees, his research interests include bee biology, pollination ecology, foraging behaviour and management of bee populations, and systematics and ecology of bees with an emphasis on the genus *Bombus*. He is actively involved in issues related to vernal pool pollination, urban bee gardens, native bee pollination of crops, and bumble bee decline.

✉ Professor Emeritus, Department of Entomology, University of California, One Shields Avenue, Davis, CA 95616-8584, USA

☎ +1-(530) 752-0482

📠 +1-(530) 754-7757

🖥 rwthorp@ucdavis.edu

Masahiro Mitsuhata is a researcher in the Integrated Pest Management team at ArystaLifeScience, Japan. He is a pollination specialist and technical advisor on bumble bees. He researches foraging behaviour and the effect of bumble bee pollination on crops. His work has made a significant contribution to the commercialization of Japanese native bumble bees. He is actively involved in the spread of scientific-based education on the usage of commercialized native bumble bees.

✉ Bio Systems, Integrated Pest Management Project, Japan, Asia and the Life Science Business Group, Arysta LifeScience Corporation, 8-1, Akashi-cho, Chuo-ku, Tokyo 104-6591, Japan

☎ +81-3-3547-4415

🖥 masahiro.mitsuhata@arysta.com

Marius Wasbauer is research associate at the Bohart Museum of Entomology at University of California, Davis. He is an internationally recognised authority on spider wasps (Pompilidae), tiphiid wasps and other solitary wasps. Formerly with the California Department of Food and Agriculture as senior scientist, Insect Biosystematics, he was first to identity the presence of Africanised honey bees ('killer bees') in California and participated in the subsequent statewide eradication efforts.

✉ Research Associate, Bohart Museum of Entomology 1124 Academic Surge, University of California, Davis, CA 95616 USA

☎ +1-(541) 469-3152

📠 +1-(541) 469-3152

🖥 mwasb@600amps.com

CORPORATE SOCIAL RESPONSIBILITY (CSR) HAS been defined as 'the efforts corporations make above and beyond regulation to balance the needs of stakeholders with the need to make a profit' (Doane 2005: 23). As part of CSR, businesses have placed increasing emphasis on understanding and managing the impact of their activities on the natural environment (Dyllick and Hockerts 2002). Indeed, CSR, which has boomed in Japan since 2003 (Tanimoto 2012), has come to embody the notion of the 'triple bottom line' where companies are increasingly expected to take to heart issues of environmental and social sustainability in addition to sustainability of corporate profits (Fukukawa and Teramoto 2009). This has developed largely in response to pressures from environmentalists, scientists, NGOs, and other key stakeholders of the firm including shareholders, employees, and clients (Tanimoto 2004, 2012; Waddock *et al.* 2002).

Biodiversity, however, is a relatively unfamiliar concept in the corporate lexicon, and comparatively little attention has been given to the effects of business on biodiversity and ecosystem health despite the fundamental role of biodiversity in human well-being (Winn and Pogutz 2013). We propose that biodiversity is a CSR challenge largely because it is so poorly understood, and that Japan is emerging as a role model in its stakeholder approach to biodiversity protection through balancing commercial interests and ecological concerns, as illustrated by the global bumble bee trade.

Japanese firms have long been concerned with the natural environment (Fukukawa and Moon 2004; Horiuchi and Nakamura 2001; Tanimoto 2004). This is evident, for instance, in Japan's Global Environment Charter which was established in 1991 by Keidanren (Nippon Keidanren as of 2002), Japan's primary business group, to guide member companies on environmental issues. Prompted by the pollution problems in the high-growth 1960s and the two oil crises of the 1970s, an appeal was made to member companies to put Japan's highly developed technology to work to safeguard the environment. The voluntary guidelines for corporate action encourage member companies to protect ecosystems and conserve resources, protect the global environment and improve the local living environment, ensure the environmental soundness of products, and protect the health and safety of employees and citizens (Keidanren 1991).

Nevertheless, voluntary guidelines may not be enough, particularly when it comes to environmental protection (e.g. Horiuchi and Nakamura 2001). Tanimoto (2012), while noting the value of voluntary CSR action by firms, questions whether the efforts of individual firms will automatically translate to sustainable development of the entire socio-economic system. As we will discuss below, the Global Environment Charter guidelines provide a baseline for environment-related CSR efforts but legislation was ultimately enacted to further protect biodiversity in Japan. This required stakeholder involvement of the government, firms, scientists, environmentalists, and the general public.

Bridging the management, sustainability, and entomology literature, we present an example of the complexities involved with biodiversity protection and the relationship to CSR. We begin with an overview of biodiversity as a CSR challenge, the case of the global bumble bee trade, and ramifications for biodiversity.

Next, we consider Japan's stakeholder approach to balancing commercial interests and ecological concerns, and conclude with implications for CSR.

Biodiversity as a CSR challenge

Biodiversity refers to the 'variety of genes, species, and ecosystems that constitute life on Earth', and allows for the provision of numerous essential services to society (Rands *et al.* 2010: 1298). Essential services include the provision of material goods such as food and nonmaterial benefits such as recreation. It also includes the provision of pollination and pest control services to agriculture, and longer term resilience to disturbance in the environment and agricultural change (Rands *et al.* 2010). Biodiversity involves interactions among organisms and with the physical environment, that is, soil, water, and air. The resilience of an ecosystem, and its ability to adapt to changing conditions, is aided through reservoirs of biodiversity (Slootweg 2005; Rands *et al.* 2010). The loss of biodiversity, in the form of shrinkage or disappearance of genes and species, means that ecosystem services are diminished or compromised. A loss of biodiversity leads to unstable ecosystems and life support processes become unreliable (Slootweg 2005).

Biodiversity has been rapidly declining in recent years (Ehrlich and Pringle 2008; Winn and Pogutz 2013). The key drivers of biodiversity loss include human population growth, international trade, economic specialisation, and invasive species. Continued growth of the human population results in the increased demand for consumption, and for land development to create living space. It also results in the intensification of agriculture to accommodate higher demand for food products (Ehrlich and Pringle 2008). International trade, and complex networks of supply chains, contributes to loss of biodiversity worldwide through the spread of disease, parasites, and invasive species (Korhonen 2006; Lenzen *et al.* 2012). Invasive species, or the introduction of non-native species into local ecosystems, pose one of the greatest threats to biodiversity worldwide (Graystock *et al.* 2013). The introduction of non-native species through international trade can result in predatory behaviour, competition with native species, and the disruption of ecosystem relationships such as the unique pollinating activity between particular species of insects and plants (e.g. Ehrlich and Pringle 2008; Goka 1998). These effects can threaten the existence of native species and compromise the health of local ecosystems by reducing future evolutionary potential and ecosystem resilience and sustainability (Ehrlich and Pringle 2008).

Biodiversity poses a challenge to CSR, we believe, because of its indirect linkages to business activity, lack of visibility, and difficulty in being understood (Rands *et al.* 2010; Winn and Pogutz 2013). Biodiversity loss can, of course, be visible and result from direct effects of business on the environment such as the loss of marine life from an oil spill. Corporate responsibility is evident in such a case. It is more difficult to ascertain the indirect effects of business on the environment, especially when they have low visibility and are diffused on a global scale (Horiuchi and Nakamura 2001). Examples include global warming and biodiversity loss such as insects and plants. It is not uncommon for companies to be sceptical of their indirect links to environmental damage and to demand sufficient scientific evidence before acknowledging responsibility. As a result, the burden of proof is generally placed on the scientific community so that environmental degradation such as biodiversity loss often goes unrecognised as a responsibility of firms.

The example that we highlight in this paper is the indirect effects of business on bumble bee species. Bumble bees have an important role as pollinators. About 8% of the world's known 250,000 species of flowering plants rely exclusively on bumble bees for pollination (Buchmann and Nabhan 1996). Flowering plants around the world include food crops and some that provide fibre, drugs, and fuel. Bee species have disappeared in some countries, and are under threat of decline in various other countries of the world including Japan. This has far reaching implications for biodiversity due to the role of native bees as pollinators of indigenous flora with consequences for present and future generations. A number of reasons have been proposed by scientists, including exposure to pesticides, loss of suitable habitat, climate change, and the transmission of diseases and parasites through the international transport of bumble bees for commercial purposes (Goka et al. 2001; Thorp 2003, Winter et al. 2006). The global bumble bee trade is presented in the next section and used to illustrate the complex relationships between business and biodiversity, the challenge that biodiversity poses to CSR, and Japan's approach to addressing these issues.

The global bumble bee trade

Economic benefits

The commercial bumble bee rearing business had its beginnings in 1985 with the discovery by a Belgian veterinarian of the value of using the Eurasian bumble bee *Bombus terrestris* for the pollination of greenhouse tomatoes (Velthuis and van Doorn 2006). Bumble bees pollinate a range of crops and are particularly effective pollinators of tomatoes. Compared with the traditional hormone or mechanical pollination for greenhouse crops, bumble bee pollination is cheaper, more natural, leads to higher fruit quality and more abundant fruit, and results in better prices (Velthuis and van Doorn 2006).

The commercial bumble bee trade has developed substantially since 1985 in tandem with a heightened demand for greenhouse crop pollination, particularly tomatoes. The ability to produce bumble bee colonies year-round facilitated the global expansion of the tomato greenhouse industry by providing a more cost effective method of pollinating the crop. There are now over 30 producers worldwide, with most of the market share covered by three companies: Biobest of Belgium, and Koppert Biological Systems and Bunting Brinkman Bees, both of the Netherlands. Several species of bumble bee are mass-reared and exported on a commercial basis to provide pollination services for agricultural crops. The main species is the Eurasian *Bombus terrestris,* commonly called the large earth bumble bee. It is indigenous to Europe, coastal North Africa, and West and Central Asia. This bee can now be found on every continent as a result of its global trade.

The large earth bumble bee was introduced into Japan in 1991 for experimental purposes (Kanbe *et al.* 2008), and in 1992 for greenhouse crop pollination (Ono and Wada 1996; Inari *et al.* 2005). The companies that distribute bumble bee colonies in Japan are BioBest, Cats Agrisystems, Koppert (associated with Arysta LifeScience Corporation, formerly Tomen Corporation), Tokaibussan Co., Ltd, and API Company, Ltd. Despite the economic benefits of the industry to provide a natural and cost-effective pollination service for greenhouse crops, there are ecological concerns associated with the industry when the bees escape from greenhouses and interact with indigenous bees and plants (e.g. Goka 2010).

Ecological concerns

Entomologists from Japan and other countries have raised concerns about the harmful ecological effects of the large earth bumble bee (and other introduced bumble bees) on the flora and fauna of local ecosystems. The following summarises the main entomological research findings.

Competition for foraging and nesting
The introduction of the large earth bumble bee has been found to compete with native bumble bees for foraging and nesting sites in Japan (Inoue *et al.* 2008; Nagamitsu *et al.* 2007). Research findings indicate that the large earth bumble bee has a rapid rate of reproduction that could potentially displace native bees from foraging and nest sites. These findings substantiate research done in other parts of the world.

Disruption of pollinating behaviour
The introduction of the large earth bumble bee has been found by Japanese entomologists to disrupt the pollinating behaviour of native bumble bee species, resulting in a decrease of nectar availability and consequent reduction in seed production (Dohzono *et al.* 2008; Kenta *et al.* 2007). The results suggest that bumble bee-pollinated native plants are relatively specialised to native bumble bee pollinators.

Reproductive disturbance and genetic contamination
Japanese entomologists have found evidence that interbreeding between non-native and native species may lead to reproductive disturbance and genetic contamination of native bumble bee species (e.g. Tsuchida *et al.* 2010). A laboratory examination of interbreeding revealed a low hatching rate of eggs; further, the eggs were found to be inviable due to genetic mechanisms which prevent normal egg development (Kanbe *et al.* 2008). Similar results of introduced commercial bumble bees have been obtained in other parts of the world.

Transmission of parasites and diseases

Perhaps the greatest concern with the transport of bumble bees across international borders, or otherwise outside of their natural distribution range, is the transmission of parasites and disease to native bumble bees. In Japan, tracheal mites have been detected in imported bumble bee colonies (Goka *et al.* 2001), and the presence of microsporidian pathogens in these bees have been determined to infect native species of bumble bees (Niwa *et al.* 2004). Similar findings have been observed in other parts of the world, for instance in the United States (Thorp 2003), Mexico (Winter *et al.* 2006), Argentina (Arbetman *et al.* 2013), and the United Kingdom (Graystock *et al.* 2013).

The above research findings suggest that the global trade in commercial bumble bees has introduced invasive species into countries around the world, with implications for biodiversity loss. The findings underscore concerns that introduced non-native bumble bees may contribute to the decline or disappearance of some local species of bumble bee. The following section describes how these findings have resulted in protective legislation in Japan and informed Japanese business behaviour.

A 'balancing act' of stakeholders

Legislative framework

As referred to earlier, the Global Environment Charter was established as a set of voluntary guidelines for Japanese firms to safeguard the environment while pursuing their business objectives. In some areas of business endeavour, voluntary guidelines may not be adequate to protect the environment (Horiuchi and Nakamura 2001). This is not to say that businesses are necessarily negligent, but may not be fully aware of the implications of their actions on the environment (Etzion 2007; Tanimoto 2004). This was deemed the case with regard to the import of non-native wildlife.

In 2001, the Cabinet Office executed a public opinion poll that showed a growing public concern about imported non-native species of plants and animals. In 2002, the New National Biodiversity Strategy was adopted, and alien species was identified as a critical factor affecting biodiversity which needed immediate attention. In 2003, a three-year plan for promoting regulation reform was initiated by the Cabinet, in which the issue of alien species was considered. It was acknowledged that there was no law that dealt with the conservation of biodiversity, and that 'the public and business sectors do not fully understand the problem of alien species' (MOE 2004b).

In March 2004, the Japanese Cabinet submitted a bill dealing with Invasive Alien Species (IAS) to the Diet (the national legislature of Japan). The bill was introduced to prevent adverse effects on ecosystems, human safety, agriculture, forestry and fisheries caused by IAS. The Diet passed the bill without amendments and the Invasive Alien Species Act was promulgated on 2 June 2004; enforcement of the law began on 1 June 2005 (MOE 2007). The law prohibits the raising, planting, storing or carrying, importing and other handling of IAS, with the exception of specified cases that require permission of the relevant authorities and securing IAS under special facilities. Substantial penalties are imposed on both individuals and corporations for violation of the law. The Invasive Alien Species Act stipulates that persons shall be imprisoned for up to three years and/or fined up to 3 million yen (MOE 2004a).

The large earth bumble bee (*Bombus terrestris*) was added to the list of invasive alien species in 2006 (MOE 2007). Importation is prohibited without permission from the competent ministers. When permitted, a protective covering must be placed over the greenhouses so that the bees cannot escape. The two ministries most involved are the Ministry of the Environment (MOE) and the Ministry of Agriculture, Forestry and Fisheries (MAFF). MAFF has strong lobbies within the farming communities. The core of Japanese agriculture is formed by many small farming households structured into producers' cooperatives, which are overseen by MAFF. MOE has good working relations with scientists and conservationists. Entomologists made their research findings known to MOE about the harmful effects of the imported large earth bumble bee. Thus, the fate of the large earth bumble bee became caught between those who support agricultural productivity and those who support conservationism (see Goka 2010 for a detailed review of politics and process surrounding the designation of this bumble bee as an invasive species).

Japan's legislation is relatively unique in that it balances commercial needs with ecological concerns (Goka 2010). Generally, fauna or flora that are designated as invasive species are prohibited. In the United States, for instance, the Eurasian large earth bumble bee is completely banned, and an indigenous species has been developed for commercial use. The current regulatory challenge in the US is the intra-country transport of native bumble bees, where bees indigenous to one part of the country are thought to be harmful to bees in other parts of the country (Thorp 2003; Winter *et al.* 2006). In the case of Australia, the large earth bumble bee is not formally banned at the national level, yet the Australian Hydroponic and Greenhouse Association was denied an application to import the large earth bumble bee. This decision was apparently influenced by the bee being listed as a threatening species in two Australian states (Moore and Gross 2012). The large earth bumble bee is traded throughout Eurasia where it is native. However, there is growing concern among European entomologists about the spread of parasites (e.g. Graystock *et al.* 2013) and the effects of the various Eurasian subspecies of this bumble bee on local European ecosystems (e.g. Kraus *et al.* 2013). By contrast to the above examples, Japan has a permission system established by MOE whereby farmers can import the banned large earth bumble bee if they can demonstrate that their greenhouses are secure with netting (Yoneda *et al.* 2007). At the same time, MAFF has advocated the commercial rearing of indigenous bumble bees as an alternative to the Eurasian large earth bumble bee (Goka 2010). In this way, the stakeholder process and resulting legislation in Japan has balanced the interests of conservationists and businesses.

Impact on business behaviour

The global bumble bee-rearing suppliers have begun to shift production to colonies of indigenous Japanese bumble bees for use in Japan. In fact, some companies have been in the process of researching the use of indigenous bees for the pollination of greenhouse plants long before the promulgation of the Invasive Species Act of 2004 and addition of the large earth bumble bee in 2006. According to Mitsuhata (2006), Arysta LifeScience Corporation, for instance, succeeded in increasing colonies of an indigenous bumble bee (*Bombus ignitus*) to commercial quantities as far back as 1999. Other companies such as Biobest and Tokaibussan Co., Ltd have also been in the process of replacing colonies of the large earth bumble bee with colonies of an indigenous species for use in Japan. This can be attributed to the findings from early investigations of the large earth bumble bee by Japanese entomologists (Goka 1998; Ono 1997) and a lengthy stakeholder dialogue process that resulted in legislation that balances business, social, and environmental concerns.

On the demand side, greenhouse crop growers have begun to use indigenous species, although the preference for the large earth bumble bee remains strong. The large earth bumble bee is a hearty, 'industrial' bumble bee that provides consistent, high-yielding crops. Educational efforts have been under way through the producer cooperatives, where the ecological risks of using the large earth bumble bee are discussed (Goka 2010). Training is also given on the securing of greenhouses when using the large earth bumble bee, since the practice in small farming businesses has been to use one colony to pollinate several, clustered tomato greenhouses where the bees are allowed to freely move between greenhouse enclosures (Ishii *et al.* 2008). The use of indigenous bees has been endorsed by large companies such as Kagome Company, Ltd that entered the fresh tomato business following agricultural reforms in 2001 (JETRO 2005). Kagome, one of the biggest food companies in Japan and the largest tomato processor in the Pacific Rim, has tomato-growing contracts with multiple corporations and farms. Interviews at Kagome by one of the authors confirmed that the company is encouraging its agricultural partners to use indigenous bees as an environmental safety precaution.

In sum, the legislation that restricts importation of the large earth bumble bee grew out of concerns by entomologists that biodiversity and ecosystem health in Japan was being compromised. Japan's legislation balances commercial interests and ecological concerns in a way that supports businesses to be responsible to the environment by changing business behaviours that had unintended consequences for local ecosystems.

Discussion

We have proposed that biodiversity is a CSR challenge, and that Japan is emerging as a role model on the global stage in addressing this challenge. Biodiversity protection poses a challenge for businesses to assume responsibility for their actions because the impacts are often indirect, have low visibility and unfold over time, perhaps generations. The commercial bumble bee trade provides a focal point to examine the complexities of biodiversity and the role of various stakeholders in bringing low-visibility issues to the fore and forging clearer pathways of responsibility for corporations and small businesses. The unfolding of developments in the commercial bumble bee trade, leading up to and following the designation of the large earth bumble bee as an invasive species, is indicative of the challenges that biodiversity protection poses to businesses. It is a concrete example of how the scientific community, government, and businesses worked together toward biodiversity protection while supporting commercial interests. Japan's approach has positive CSR implications because of the adoption of the precautionary principle, the breadth and integration of stakeholder engagement, and stakeholder outcomes that balance the interests of conservationists and businesses.

The precautionary principle is an operating guideline of the Convention on Biological Diversity (CBD 2004). Applicable to firms and government authorities alike, it means to act in a precautionary manner even when the cause and effect linkages between business activity and environmental damage have not been fully established (CBD 2004). This is particularly relevant when considering biodiversity because the complexity of ecosystems is so poorly understood. Another aspect of the precautionary principle is that all relevant sectors of society and scientific disciplines should be involved in, and cooperate toward, addressing challenges related to maintaining biodiversity and the health of ecosystems (CBD 2004). In other words, stakeholder engagement is important.

Japan's Global Environment Charter of 1991 set forth a broad guideline for companies to work with key stakeholders such as the government, community, NGOs, scientists, and overseas organisations to preserve the environment. However, it was specific government regulation in the form of the Invasive Alien Species Act that subsequently limited the importation of the large earth bumble bee. The Invasive Alien Species Act came into being with input from various stakeholders including corporations, scientists, and the general public. Articles of the Invasive Species Act call for collaboration among stakeholders and the sharing of information. This includes allowing scientific research to be conducted on company activities, reporting results to government authorities and international agencies and NGOs. The Act also identifies public education as a significant priority. The Act is consistent with the operating guidelines offered by the Convention on Biological Diversity (CBD 2004). The CBD specifies that all relevant sectors of society and scientific disciplines should be involved in, and cooperate toward, addressing challenges related to maintaining biodiversity and the health of ecosystems. Indeed, the breadth of Japan's stakeholder engagement spans a full range of actors from the grass-roots community level to the Imperial Household.

Japan's regulation of the large earth bumble bee has been heralded by entomologists in other parts of the world as an important step to protecting biodiversity not only in Japan, but globally. Indeed, Japanese entomologists were among the early investigators of the ecological effects of the large earth bumble bee (e.g. Goka 1998; Ono 1997) and a substantial amount of research has been undertaken in Japan. These studies are increasingly cited globally as the ecological concern with invasive bumble bees becomes more evident in other countries (e.g. Graystock *et al.* 2013). At the same time, agricultural businesses are able to continue using a commercially desirable bumble bee while exercising precaution, experimenting with the use of indigenous bees, and cooperating with scientists. Tomato-growing enterprises in Hokkaido and elsewhere in Japan have allowed entomologists to conduct research on their bumble bee pollination activities, as evidenced by the plethora of research papers in recent years. Indicative of the range of stakeholder engagement, beyond that of scientists, businesses, and government as described above, community volunteers have monitored the extent of alien bumble bees in rural areas and contributed to research efforts (Kojima 2006). Further, a televised visit by the Emperor and Empress of Japan to the National Institute for Environmental Studies to discuss longer-term global environmental concerns, including invasive species and the deterioration of ecosystems, provided recognition of the importance of these issues (NIES 2013).

If we reconsider our operating definition of corporate social responsibility as 'the efforts corporations make above and beyond regulation to balance the needs of stakeholders with the need to make a profit' (Doane 2005: 23), one may question whether the outcome would have been different without the Invasive Species Act. Would companies have listened to the concerns of scientists, acted in a precautionary manner, and changed their business behaviour? Research has shown that firms generally tend to be more 'responsible' when government regulation is in place. While a survey of corporate efforts that go above what is required by legislation is beyond the scope of this paper, there are indications that companies and small businesses in Japan are making such efforts. The legislation prohibits the import of the large earth bumble bee, though gives some 'slack' to companies by allowing the import under certain conditions, thus balancing environmental and commercial concerns. Yet, companies are going beyond what is legally mandated by experimenting with, and promoting, the use of indigenous bumble bee species as an eventual replacement for the large earth bumble bee for commercial pollination in Japan. This is an acknowledgement not only of the seriousness of biodiversity loss but of the responsibility that all stakeholders have in its prevention.

Firms can no longer deny their impact on the environment and their responsibility for its protection (Tanimoto 2004). We have illustrated the CSR challenge of protecting biodiversity while meeting commercial interests. The key message to managers is that: 1) the CSR challenges related to biodiversity are often invisible to corporate actors; 2) the challenges are voiced by scientists so it is important to keep abreast of the scientific debate; and 3) the ultimate solution to these challenges is likely to be a synthesis of various stakeholder interests, so being prepared to collaborate with different stakeholder groups, such as providing access to data, should be beneficial. While culture may shape the process of stakeholder engagement (Lalor and Hickey 2014), and specific biodiversity issues and their solutions will differ, we believe that the above message is generally applicable to businesses anywhere. This is equally true, we believe, even if a particular biodiversity issue is not readily quantifiable in economic terms. After all, ecosystems and their biodiversity play a vital role in the provision of products and services that sustain and enhance human life, whether or not they are known, recognised or quantified. The full value of biodiversity to mankind is yet to be discovered. The loss of biodiversity, including insect populations, has far reaching consequences for present and future generations. Striking the right balance between biodiversity protection and commercial activities that together serve humankind, as Japan's businesses, government agencies, scientists, and other actors have demonstrated through a process of stakeholder engagement, appears to be a new wave of corporate social responsibility.

References

Arbetman, M.P., Meeus, I., Morales, C.L., Aizen, M.A., and Smagghe, G. (2013), 'Alien parasite hitchhikes to Patagonia on invasive bumblebee', *Biological Invasions* 15: 489-494.

Asada, S. and Ono, M. (1996), 'Tomato pollination with Japanese native bumblebees (*Bombus* spp.)', ISHS *Acta Horticulturae* 437: VII International Symposium on Pollination.

Buchmann, S. L. and Nabhan, G. P. (1996), *The Forgotten Pollinators.* Washington, DC, Island Press.

CBD, Convention on Biological Diversity (2004), Decision V/6 Ecosystem Approach. Decision VII/11 Ecosystem Approach. Retrieved March 25, 2014 from http://www.biodiv.org/decisions/default.aspx?m=COP-07&id=7748&Ig=0.

Doane, D. (2005), 'The myth of CSR', *Stanford Social Innovation Review*, Stanford Graduate School of Business, Fall 2005, pp. 23-29.

Dohzono, I., Kunitake, Y.K., Yokoyama, J., and Goka, K. (2008), 'Alien bumblebee affects native plant reproduction through interactions with native bumblebees', *Ecology*, 89(11): 3082-3092.

Dyllick, T. and Hockerts, K. (2002), 'Beyond the business case for corporate sustainability', *Business Strategy and the Environment*, 11(2): 130-141.

Ehrlich, P. and Pringle, R.M. (2008), 'Where does biodiversity go from here? A grim business-as-usual forecast and a hopeful portfolio of partial solutions', *Proceedings of the National Academy of Science*, 105, 11579-11586.

Etzion, D. (2007), 'Research on organizations and the natural environment, 1992–present: A review', *Journal of Management*, 33(4), 637-664.

Fukukawa, K. and Moon, J. (2004), 'A Japanese model of corporate social responsibility? A study of website reporting', *Journal of Corporate Citizenship*, 16: 45-59.

Fukukawa, K. and Teramoto, Y. (2009), 'Understanding Japanese CSR: The reflections of managers in the field of global operations', *Journal of Business Ethics*, 85(1): 133-146.

Goka, K. (1998), 'Influence of invasive species on native species: will the European bumblebee, *Bombus terrestris*, bring genetic pollution into the Japanese native species?' *Bulletin of Biogeographical Society of Japan*, 53: 91-101.

Goka, K. (2010), 'Introduction to the special feature for ecological risk assessment of introduced bumblebees: Status of the European bumblebee, *Bombus terrestris*, in Japan as a beneficial pollinator and an invasive alien species', *Applied Entomology and Zoology*, 45: 1-6.

Goka, K., Okabe, K., Yoneda, M. and Niwa, S. (2001), 'Bumblebee commercialization will cause worldwide migration of parasitic mites', *Molecular Ecology*, 10: 2095-2099.

Graystock, P.,Yates, K., Evison, S.E.F., Darvill, B., Goulson, D., and Hughs, W.O.H. (2013), 'The Trojan hives: Pollinator pathogens, imported and distributed in bumblebee colonies', *Journal of Applied Ecology* 50(5): 1207-1215.

Horiuchi, K., and Nakamura, M. (2001), 'Environmental issues and Japanese firms', in Masao Nakamura (ed.) *The Japanese Business and Economic System: History and Prospects for the 21st Century*, New York, NY: Palgrave, pp. 364-384.

Inari, N., Nagamitsu, T., Kenta, T., Goka, K., and Hiura, T. (2005), 'Spatial and temporal pattern of introduced *Bombus terrestris* abundance in Hokkaido, Japan, and its potential impact on native bumblebees', *Population Ecology*, 47: 77-82.

Inoue, M.N., Yokoyama, J., and Washitani, I. (2008), 'Displacement of Japanese native bumblebees by the recently introduced *Bombus terrestris* (L.) (Hymenoptera: Apidae)', *Journal of Insect Conservation*, 12(2): 135-146.

Ishii, H.S., Kadoya, T., Kikuchi, R., Suda, S-I. and Washitani, I. (2008), 'Habitat and flower resource partitioning by an exotic and three native bumble bees in central Hokkaido, Japan', *Biological Conservation*, 141: 2597-2607.

JETRO (2005), 'More enterprises move into agricultural sector'. Japan External Trade Organization. Retrieved March 27, 2014 from http://www.jetro.go.jp/en/reports/ market/pdf/2005_15_h.pdf

Kanbe, Y., Okada, I., Yoneda, M., Goka, K. and Tsuchida, K. (2008), 'Interspecific mating of the introduced bumblebee *Bombus terrestris* and the native Japanese *Bombus hypoctrita sapporoensis* results in inviable hybrids', *Naturwissenschaften*, 95: 1003-1008.

Keidanren (1991), 'Guidelines for corporate action', *Global Environment Charter*. Tokyo: Keidanren. Retrieved March 27, 2014 from http://www.keidanren.or.jp/english/speech/ spe001/s01001/s01b.html.

Kenta, T., Inari, N., Nagamitsu, T., Goka, K., and Hiura, T. (2007), 'Commercialized European bumblebee can cause pollination disturbance: An experiment on seven native plant species in Japan', *Biological Conservation*, 134: 298-309.

Kraus, F.B., Szentgyorgyi, H., Rozej, E., Rhode, M., Moron, D., Woyciechowski, M., and Moritz, R.F.A. (2011), 'Greenhouse bumblebees (*Bombus terrestris*) spread their genes into the wild', *Conservation Genetics*, 12: 187-192.

Kremen, C., Williams, N.M., and Thorp, R.W. (2002), 'Crop pollination from native bees at risk from agricultural intensification', *Proceedings of the National Academy of Science (USA)*, 99: 16812-16816.

Kojima, N. (2006), 'Collaborating with volunteer citizens to the exclusion of an invasive alien bumblebee *Bombus terrestris*', *Japanese Journal of Conservation Ecology*, 11(1): 61-69.

Kokuvo, M., Toquenaga, Y., and Goka, K. (2008), 'Estimating colony number of *Bombus terrestris* (Hymenoptera, Apidae) queens foraging in Biratori, Hokkaido, Japan', *Applied Entomology and Zoology*, 43(1): 19-23.

Korhonen, J. (2006), 'On the paradox of corporate social responsibility: how can we use social science and natural science for a new vision?' *Business Ethics: A European Review*, 15(2): 200-214.

Lalor, B.M. and Hickey, G.M. (2014), 'Strengthening the role of science in environmental decision-making processes of executive government', *Organization and Environment*, 27(2): 161-180.

Lenzen, M., Moran, D., Kanemoto, K., Foran, B., Lobefaro, L. and Geschke, A. (2012), 'International trade drives biodiversity threats in developing nations', *Nature*, 486: 109-112.

Malovics, G., Csigene, N.N. and Kraus, S. (2008), 'The role of corporate social responsibility in strong sustainability', *The Journal of Socio-Economics*, 37: 907-918.

Matsumura, C., Yokoyama, J., and Washitani, I. (2004), 'Invasion status and potential ecological impacts of an invasive alien bumblebee, *Bombus terrestris* L. (Hymenoptera: Apidae) naturalized in southern Hokkaido, Japan', *Global Environmental Research*, 8(1): 51-66.

Mitsuhata, M. (2006), 'Utilization of the Japanese native bumble bee species, *Bombus ignitus*', *Agricultural Chemicals Guide*, (111). Retrieved March 27, 2014 from http://www .agrofrontier.com/guide/t_111c.htm.

MOE (2004a), Invasive Alien Species Act (Law No. 78), Tokyo: Ministry of the Environment, Government of Japan. Retrieved March 27, 2014 from http://www.env.go.jp/en/nature/ as/040427.pdf

MOE (2004b), Measures to be taken against Invasive Alien Species in Japan, Tokyo: Ministry of the Environment, Government of Japan. Retrieved March 27, 2014 from http://www.env.go.jp/en/nature/as/040326.pdf

MOE (2007), *Annual Report on the Environment and the Sound Material-Cycle Society in Japan 2007*, Tokyo: Ministry of the Environment, Government of Japan.

Moore, C., and Gross, C. (2012), 'Great big hairy bees! Regulating the European Bumblebee, *Bombus terrestris* L. What does it say about the Precautionary Principle?' *International Journal of Rural Law and Policy*, Occasional Paper Series 2012: 2-19.

Nagamitsu, T., Kenta, Inari, N., Horita, H., T., Goka, K., and Hiura, T. (2007), 'Foraging interactions between native and exotic bumblebees: Enclosure experiments using native flowering plants', *Japanese Insect Conservation*, 47: 77-82.

NIES (2013), National Institute for Environmental Studies, Japan. Retrieved March 27, 2014 from http://www.nies.go.jp/gaiyo/pamphlet/nies2013-e.pdf.

Ono, M. (1997), 'Ecological implications of introduced *Bombus terrestris*, and significance of domestication of Japanese native bumblebees (*Bombus* spp.)', *Proceedings of the International Workshop on Biological Invasions of Ecosystem by Pests and Beneficial Organisms*, National Institute of Agro-Environmental Science, Ministry of Agriculture, Forestry, and Fisheries, Japan. Tsukuba, Japan, 25-27 February 1997, pp. 244-252.

Rands, M.R.W., Adams, W.M., Bennun, L., Butchart, S.H.M., Clements, A., Coomes, D., Entwistle, A., Hodge, I., Kapos, V., Scharlemann, J.P.W., Sutherland, W.J., and Vira, B. (2010), 'Biodiversity conservation: challenges beyond 2010', *Science*, 329(5997), 1298-1303.

Slootweg, R. (2005), 'Biodiversity assessment framework: Making biodiversity part of corporate responsibility', *Impact Assessment and Project Appraisal*, 23(1): 37-46.

Tanimoto, K., (2004), 'Changes in the market society and corporate social responsibility', *Asian Business and Management*, 3(2): 151-172.

Tanimoto, K., (2012), 'Structural change in corporate society and CSR in Japan', in Fukukawa, K. (ed.) *Corporate Social Responsibility in Asia*, New York: Routledge, pp. 45-66.

Thorp, R.W. (2003), 'Bumble bees (Hymenoptera: Apidae): Commercial use and environmental concerns', in K. Strickler and J.H. Cane (eds.) *For Non-native Crops, Whence Pollinators of the Future?* Proceedings of Thomas Say Publications in Entomology. Entomological Society of America. Lanham, MD, pp. 21-40.

Tsuchida, K., Kondo, N.I., Inoue, M.N., and Goka, K. (2010), 'Reproductive disturbance risks to indigenous Japanese bumblebees from introduced *Bombus terrestris*', *Applied Entomology and Zoology*, 45: 49-58.

Velthuis, H.H.W., and van Doorn, A. (2006), 'A century of advances in bumblebee domestication and the environmental aspects of its commercialization for pollination', *Apidologie*, 37: 421-451.

Waddock, S.A., Bodwell, C., and Graves, S.B. (2002), 'Responsibility: The new business imperative', *Academy of Management Executive*, 16(2), 132-148.

Winn, M.I. and Pogutz, S. (2013), 'Business, ecosystems, and biodiversity: New horizons for management research', *Organization and Environment*, 26(2): 203-229.

Winter, K., Adams, L., Thorp, R., Inouye, D., Day, L., Ascher, J., and Buchmann, S. (2006), 'Importation of Non-Native Bumble Bees into North America: Potential Consequences of Using *Bombus terrestris* and other Non-Native Bumble Bees for Greenhouse Crop Pollination in Canada, Mexico, and the United States', A White Paper of the North American Pollinator Protection Campaign.

Yoneda, M., Yokoyama, J., Tsuchida, K., Osaki, T., Itoya, S., and Goka, K. (2007), 'Preventing *Bombus terrestris* from escaping with a net covering over a greenhouse in Hokkaido', *Japanese Journal of Applied Entomology and Zoology*, 51(1): 39-44.

DOI: [10.9774/GLEAF.8757.2014.de.00005]

Organisational Geographies and Corporate Responsibility

A Case Study of Japanese Multinational Corporations Operating in South Africa and Tanzania

Roger Levermore

Hong Kong University of Science and Technology, China

This article considers how an increasingly important aspect of multinational corporation strategy- corporate social responsibility - is influenced by 'organisational geographies'. Organisational geographies is a phrase used to explain the mixture of the confluence of geographical, cultural and organisational influences that helps shape strategy for a company. This article shows five different organisational geographies in operation by relating each to a case study of seven Japanese MNC subsidiaries in South Africa and Tanzania.

● Organisational geographies
● CSR
● Japanese MNCs
● South Africa
● Tanzania

Roger Levermore is a Senior Lecturer and Associate Director of MBA programmes at Hong Kong University of Science and Technology (2012– present). He started his academic career at the University of Liverpool in 2001 and has published widely on the way business has addressed poverty and corporate responsibility. His PhD focused on the wine and textile industries in South Africa (1998–2001). Roger also teaches on leadership, strategy and ethics.

✉ HKUST, Department of Management, School of Business Management, Clear Water Bay, Kowloon, Hong Kong

☎ +852 2358 7743

🖥 rjleverm@ust.hk

PRECISELY EXAMINING STRATEGIC DECISION-MAKING IS fraught with problems as a complete understanding of the processes is 'unknowable'
(Parsons, 1995: 1) especially in the 'inherently disordered' heterarchical
structure of multinational corporations (MNCs) (Morgan *et al.* 2003).
Despite this, social studies posits the importance of the institutional environment (internal, institutional factors such as organisational structure and different relationships that exist between departments—associated initially with
Chandler, 1962), industry clusters (see for example, Porter 2000), and political
and cultural systems (associated with Ouchi, 1980) in shaping strategy. Yet,
recognition of the role of 'organisational geography', which essentially com-
bines these elements of geography and organisational culture, is limited. This is
particularly the case for an increasingly important element of strategy, corporate
social responsibility (CSR) (Pettigrew, 2009: 13).

The term 'organisational geographies' borrows Dicken's (2005) definition
where organisational geographies are based on notions of territory and hierarchy in which networks of organisational culture and geography (local, national
and global level) play an important role in shaping an organisation's attitudes.
Networks are regarded as 'a complex circuitry with a multiplicity of linkages'
between actors and institutions inside and outside of the company that span
the spheres of politics, economy and society.

This article details five different organisational geographies in operation by
relating each to a case study of seven Japanese MNC subsidiaries in South Africa
and Tanzania (Itochu, Komatsu, Sony, Sumitomo Corporation and Toyota in
South Africa and Panasonic and Sumitomo Chemical in Tanzania). The central
thesis tested is that Japanese MNCs are most closely associated with two of these
concepts—both based on having a strongly centralised head office structure
that significantly influences the entire approach to strategy—where localised
strategy networks are marginalised. This article develops these understandings
empirically; the data drawn upon for this article derives from research projects
financed by a range of small-scale research funds that allowed for the interviewing of 34 stakeholders (representatives of MNCs, non-governmental organisations, government and governmental organisations, civil society and labour) in
Japan and South Africa who contribute to formulating CSR.

This combination of companies has been chosen because there is a sizeable
presence of Japanese trade in South Africa and Tanzania (for example, Japan
is one of South Africa's largest trading partners while South Africa is the most
important economic and strategic partner in Africa for Japan). Japanese MNCs
have played a pivotal role in recent decades in influencing management practices; they are associated with strongly centralised strategy decision-making and
an approach to CSR that focused on providing lifetime employment, advancing
training skills and supporting the social development of communities (Pascale
and Athos, 1981; Fukukawa and Moon, 2004). Even if the perception of Japanese
management falls well short of the ethical organisation detailed by MacIntyre
(1984) (particularly following mounting criticism of Japanese corporate ethics),
given the immensity of their impact on global trade management practice, an
examination of their current management style through the implementation of

CSR in South Africa and Tanzania merits attention, especially at a time when the Japanese government is encouraging multinationals to intensify trade in sub-Saharan Africa because of the need to acquire natural resources.

Five organisational geographies

This article notes that there are five types of organisational geographies that shape CSR strategy that are linked to the seminal work of Bartlett and Ghoshal (1998). The first three are based on MNC typologies that highlight organisational geographies influenced largely by centralised strategic management approaches, in which the head office determines CSR throughout the organisation. They are:

▶ **Global firm stakeholder CSR approach.** Global networks shape the practice of CSR that has characteristics associated with embracing Western, individualistic notions of responsibility (human rights, the environment, labour standards, and poverty reduction)

▶ **Global firm shareholder approach.** Global networks shape reactionary approaches to CSR; this is linked to the 'shareholder' perspective that sees little significant value to CSR

▶ **International firm approach.** Where 'home nation' local networks—in the head office country—are a significant influence on how CSR is viewed and implemented

Two other conceptualisations denote that MNCs have strategic management structures that are influenced to varying degrees by organisational geographies that highlight the strength of local networks based in subsidiary countries. These are:

▶ **Multidomestic firm approach.** The MNC strategy network is receptive to local understandings of CSR exerted in the countries of operation

▶ **Transnational firm approach.** Modern MNCs are influenced by a hybrid and hierarchical pressure by local and global networks

In relation to these five organisational geographies, few analysts indicate that many Japanese MNCs relate to a transnational conceptualisation of corporate governance. Morgan *et al.* (2003) suggest that Japanese financial institutions in the 1980s also adhered to traits of 'transnational social spaces'. Tanimoto (undated) implies in his work that global and local influences are occasionally discernible, with Fujitsu, NEC and Matsushita sometimes labelled transnational firms. Instead, the international firm typology is more prevalent. For example, 57 of the 64 Japanese MNCs examined by Collinson and Rugman (2008) adhered to international firm characteristics because 80% or more of their trade was based in Japan. Yet, some of these could still be categorised as global firms (Segal-Horn and Faulkner, 1999: 148) having more in common with stakeholder than shareholder concepts of CSR (West, 2006). Therefore, Japanese MNCs are perceived to tend to fit into one of. Companies from the manufacturing industry with a vertical organisational structure are more likely to display characteristics associated with a **global stakeholder** company. MNCs that are from the general trading chain of Japanese companies are much more likely to be associated with an **international firm** approach to CSR. Of course, such neatly drawn lines vary in business practice; international firms do show signs of global norms. Global stakeholder firms have made a virtue of their Japanese heritage, which shows the historical commitment to CSR. Both categories of firms also show limited evidence of displaying multidomestic, global shareholder and transnational traits in the practice and strategy of CSR. For example, Toyota, due to its length and extent of operation in South Africa, comes closest to operating what might be regarded as a transnational CSR operation. So, while there is empirical evidence that relates both to Coe *et al.* (2008) and Palmer and O'Kane (2007) in so far as to which national and global networks are at play, this article also emphasises the new theoretical turn called for by Hughes *et al.* (2007) that is required to address the fluid nature of networks in appreciating the inability to clarify the organisational geographies in a homogeneous manner.

The following section therefore contextualises the CSR characteristics of Japanese MNCs operating in South Africa and Tanzania to trace the extent to which the categories outlined on CSR can be applied to this context.

Case study of Japanese MNCs in South Africa and Tanzania

Table 1 lists the seven Japanese MNCs that were selected for the research undertaken. It also documents how the companies have been categorised by their overall approach to strategic management and their size of operation globally and in South Africa.

Table 1 Summary of Japanese MNC CSR

Sources: Official head office and subsidiary company reporting of CSR and interviews with company officials in Japan and South Africa

Name of company	Details of overall operation	Details of trade and CSR activity in South Africa and Tanzania	How strategy network approach is conceptualised and operationalised
Itochu	An international firm infused with a strong regional approach as outlined by Collinson and Rugman (2008) Operates in over 80 countries and has 30,000+ employees. General trading company with seven division companies; has over 1000 subsidiaries.	Johannesburg branch started in late 1960s; 4-5% of Itochu overall trade comes from sub-Saharan Africa Owns a subsidiary – ITW along with a Black Economic Empowerment partner (2007). Invested R350 million to support the network to sell Isuzu Trucks in South Africa. Itochu also owns majority stakes in car dealerships. In 1997, invested in mining with Komatsu. However, the level of business/trade is quite minimal with 19 staff in South Africa (five of seven managers are Japanese). No CSR activities in South Africa	CSR priorities: • Supply chain dominates (makes reference to Sogo Shosha in justifying that as a priority) • Environment also a concern and social development is also referred to (pressure to consider social development strives from here and 'third party opinion'). • CSR is regarded as a promotion (PR) side of the company Extent/history of CSR reporting: • 2006 Information on organisation of CSR: • In Head Office 15 work on CSR type activities (seven in global environmental affairs; three in philanthropy; five in CSR promotion). Sits in General Affairs department (36 staff in total). • Staffed by generalists (rotate every 2/3 years). • Each division of Itochu has a CSR team. • Decision-making process is top-down. No non-Japanese staff involved. • CSR committee has no CSR division members sitting on it; Chair of Itochu, manager of General Affairs and other department heads included. • CSR taskforce has 25 members (across divisions and the seven core function areas) Global norms/awards: • Dow Jones rating. • Joined UN Global Compact in 2009 Overall categorisation? Largely international firm with shareholder tendencies and some local initiatives evident in CSR reporting.

Name of company	Details of overall operation	Details of trade and CSR activity in South Africa and Tanzania	How strategy network approach is conceptualised and operationalised
Komatsu	30,000+ employees in over three continents Construction equipment, especially for mining industry. Komatsu Ltd owns 80% and Itochu owns a 20%.	Estimated 800-1000 employees in South Africa. Focus is on construction and mining equipment as well as utility equipment (compact machines). Also supplier for Toyota. Operated in South Africa since 1961 but presence more substantial after 1997. Some CSR projects have been running since 1984: such as donations made to an ex-employee who provides craft making education skills to local community. R1.5m is spent annually on the DenRon educational project (with partner); this to be template for other schemes with other partners in South Africa such as a coal mining company from the Anglo stable in Northern Province. Ownership is 100% Japanese owned.	CR priorities: • In general, employee relations (and environment) • Strong emphasis on heritage in CSR reports. Extent/history of CSR reporting: • Environmental reports started in 2000 Information on organisation of CSR: • Head of CSR in South Africa is not an expatriate Japanese national • Head office provides little influence/ pressure for subsidiaries to enact CSR but notes a desire for branches to be involved in CSR Global norms/awards: • Member of UN Global Compact from 2008 • Member of World Business Council for Sustainable Development • Regional awards for CSR best practice including from India, Brazil and Japan Overall categorisation? Recognition of heritage, which makes Komatsu a global firm with sensitivity to local issues. This is probably because of the status of working in a 50/50 partnership with subsidiaries. This makes some aspects of the organisation multidomestic

Name of company	Details of overall operation	Details of trade and CSR activity in South Africa and Tanzania	How strategy network approach is conceptualised and operationalised
Panasonic	Involved in electronics industry such as digital AV, home appliances, industrial solutions, and other electronic and consumer products; trade primarily in Japan and Asia but has a global network of suppliers. 292,250 employees (31.3.09). 89% are in Asia.	Minute presence in Tanzania 114 employees involved in the production of dry cell batteries (since 1966) Specific CSR initiatives on top of the 'norms' inherent in the management philosophy of Panasonic (such as respect for human rights, occupational health and safety, environmental care, ethics and compliance) are minimal. The local office is an ECO Relay member and has contributed to the building of clock tower in restoration of gardens.	CSR priorities: • Environment and employee relations are strong priorities but emphasis on female empowerment and human rights included. Extent/history of CSR reporting: • Panasonic one of first Japanese companies to use the term CSR. Associated with its founder, Konosuke Matsushita in 1974 • First environmental report in 1997. • Most recent CSR reports (since 2004) are extensive. Information on organisation of CSR: • Considerable staffing levels at headquarters. 115+ in CSR related activities [5 in CSR; 30+ in philanthropy; 80+ in environmental affairs with CSR also being of importance to the HR, business compliance and occupational health offices). • The CSR department reports directly to the President's office. • Staffed by generalists but many have international experience. • CSR policy committee has ten members from across the core function areas. Meet every two months to set direction of CSR policy. • CSR in Tanzania is 'guided' by Tokyo HO but the decision is made by each site based upon the management philosophy of Panasonic. • There is also an overseas CSR enhancement team. Global norms/awards: • Not a member of the Global Compact yet. • Awarded "SAM Gold Class" in 2009 and 2010. Overall categorisation? In many ways a clear case of being a global stakeholder approach (used term 'multi-stakeholder' approach in many places).

Name of company	Details of overall operation	Details of trade and CSR activity in South Africa and Tanzania	How strategy network approach is conceptualised and operationalised
Sony	Manufacturer of electronic appliances with an estimated total workforce of 150,000	Operated since 1998 in South Africa. Currently has 141 staff (two ex-patriates). In South Africa, a few local initiatives supported (relating to education) and a large project associated with the World Cup was jointly devised, supported and run between the local and head office (evolved through a steering committee that was established to consider marketing and the World Cup).	CSR priorities: • The environment, supply chain and employee development is given prominence and so too is social development Extent/history of SR reporting: • First CSR/environmental report published in 1994 Information on organisation of CSR: • CSR department originated in 2003 • Has 11/12 staff dedicated to CSR; 2 or 3 replaced each year in revolving staff turnover. 50+ in environmental affairs department. • No CSR committee • Report directly to Senior VP. Global norms/awards: • Not a member of any but the Sony Group Code of Conduct reflects principles set out in the Organisation for Economic Co-operation and Development (OECD) Guidelines for Multinational Enterprises, the United Nations Global Compact and the United Nations Universal Declaration of Human Rights • Member of World Business Council for Sustainable Development • Awards include the Environmental Communication Awards 2006: Sustainability Excellence Award by the Global Environmental Forum. The majority of other awards granted by the Japanese government Overall categorisation? Difficult to classify; aspects relate to a global shareholder concept but also elements that are international firm and global stakeholder. The independence of the local South African office also highlights a partial multidomestic trend.

Name of company	Details of overall operation	Details of trade and CSR activity in South Africa and Tanzania	How strategy network approach is conceptualised and operationalised
Sumitomo	An international firm infused with a strong regional approach 5000 direct employees (70,755 in subsidiaries) and with a significant presence on all continents General trading company - especially mining	Minimal presence in South Africa. 33 employees in Head Office (24 South African; 9 Japanese) Has 49% of shares in Oresteel Investments Ltd, which is an iron ore and manganese mine in South Africa (which represents 2.6% of corporate group profits) CSR in South Africa is limited to corporate philanthropy (since 2009 when one of the local employees has been employed to look at CSR); one of subsidiaries is 'thinking of building a youth centre'	CSR priorities: • Dominated by employee relations. Extent/history of CSR reporting: • Extent of coverage minimal • First report 2005 Information on organisation of CSR: • 5 generalists work in CSR department and 8 work in environmental affairs. Global norms/awards: • UN Global Compact, 2009 Overall categorisation? Strongly adheres to international firm categorisation.

Name of company	Details of overall operation	Details of trade and CSR activity in South Africa and Tanzania	How strategy network approach is conceptualised and operationalised
Sumitomo Chemical	26902 employees. 126 subsidiaries. According to 2009 figures, 75% of assets are in Japan and 86% in Asia. Manufacturing company.	Limited presence in Tanzania. CSR in Africa is largely related to the business practice of producing malaria nets (increasingly through a 50/50 joint venture with a local company called A to Z textiles that was given technology free of charge). Revenue from this has contributed to construction of junior schools in East Africa.	CSR priorities: • Environment • Health • Supply chain • Social activities Extent/history of CSR reporting: • Fairly well established. 2004 – first CSR report and 1998 the first environmental report Information on organisation of CSR reporting: • Report to senior executive officer. Top down decision-making process. • Staff = 20 in responsible care department (this includes 5 working on energy and climate) and six members of CSR division (generalists) that operated as a formal department from 2010 (subsumed in general affairs before that). • The CSR department includes responsibility for corporate philanthropy. • There is also a CSR Promotion Coordinating board that promotes CSR activities in the organisation Global norms/awards: • UN Global Compact – 2005 • Member of World Business Council for Sustainable Development • Local awards for sustainability, ex. Asahi Corporate Citizenship Award Overall categorisation? A clear fit with international firm categorisation.

Name of company	Details of overall operation	Details of trade and CSR activity in South Africa and Tanzania	How strategy network approach is conceptualised and operationalised
Toyota	A global firm despite being categorised as being a triadised company by Collinson and Rugman (2008) 300,000+ worldwide in over three continents Automaker	10,000 in South Africa with R4.4m investment in infrastructure from 2003-2006. Significant operations in South Africa since 1962. Employs 7-10,000 staff and produces between 150,000 and 220,000 vehicles a year. Exports to the European market. Three local employees work on CSR; report directly to Toyota South Africa CEO Priority of CSR is largely based on education but environmental also a focus. Toyota South Africa Foundation has supported 16 schools in KwaZulu Natal since 1990.	CSR priorities: • Education • Environment • Road safety • Supply chain also noted in CSR reports Extent/history of CSR reporting: • First report in 1999 • Toyota Foundation started in 1974 Information on organisation of CSR: • Dedicated CSR and environmental affairs department from 2007 • Reports directly to President • Relates to corporate citizenship and recycling divisions Global norms/awards: • Sustainability awards granted in many area of operation including Germany, Australia and the US • Not a member of UN Global Compact but member of World Business Council for Sustainable Development Overall categorisation? Some consider Toyota to be the closest of all to being transnational. It does have major presences across continents and considers CSR based around local sensitivities and underpinned by reference to global norms.

According to the summary of concepts and overview of Japanese CSR, some of the differences expected between global and international firms are in the focus, reporting and varying influence of global and local networks. The conceptual overview of the general approaches that Japanese MNCs have shown towards CSR raises expectations that, when operating in South Africa and Tanzania, the manufacturing vertical *Keiretsu* MNCs (Komatsu, Panasonic, Sumitomo Chemical, Sony and Toyota) are more likely to highlight discernible characteristics towards CSR that are heavily ingrained with global firm traits but might also be open to some multidomestic or transnational initiatives. The general trading companies (Itochu and Sumitomo) have been categorised as being international firms by Collinson and Rugman (2008) and therefore expected to demonstrate a centralised decision-making that prioritises domestic network influence over that of the host country. Yet, some *Sogo Shosha* have developed long-established links with foreign companies, which can lead to the introduction of 'global norms', which translates to different types of CSR. Such similarities and differences were discernible in the examination of the seven MNCs researched and this section outlines where those expectations were met and where they have been contested.

Unsurprisingly, considerable substantiation affirmed that the five vertical *Keiretsu*/manufacturing MNCs confirmed their status as displaying global stakeholder approaches to CSR and similarly, the two *Sogo Shosha* highlighted their international firm CSR strategy. This was evidenced through the level and extent of CSR reporting, priorities detailed and awards conferred. As noted in the previous section, part of the reason for these differences is that the global firms all dedicate considerable resources to CSR compared with international firms. There are noticeable differences in CSR priorities between the two. All five vertical *Keiretsu* firms support global CSR initiatives infused with an individualistic orientation and all (aside from Panasonic) are either signatories of the UN Global Compact or are guided by their principles. For example, Komatsu supports specific socio-economic development initiatives, including those focused on educational programmes in South Africa. Toyota receives excellent ratings for their consideration of such global issues as respect for human rights and social development (CanPan, 2008). Panasonic refers to human rights in its CSR reporting; this has been a priority since CSR was founded in the organisation but has been given added resonance following feedback from North American and European manufacturing customers. Sony also highlights social development as one of their four pillars of CSR priorities. Furthermore, most of the global firms are aligned to the major global CSR initiatives. In contrast, the general trading companies tend to focus exclusively on Japanese CSR priorities such as the environment and supply chain. For example, international firms have only recently signed up to global initiatives (Itochu and Sumitomo in 2009). Moreover, there is some evidence to suggest that international firms are more influenced by government than are global MNCs in Japan; for instance, Sumitomo importantly explains that it is contributing to the Japanese Government's commitment to development in Africa although it should be noted that this relationship was downplayed during the interviews conducted.

In terms of CSR reporting, the five manufacturing/global firms all produced annual CSR reports that contained a considerable level of depth—and have done so for at least five years (Komatsu started environmental reporting in 2000; Panasonic, 1997; Sony, 1994; and Toyota 1999). Most also highlight the global awards they have won for their approach to CSR. For instance, Toyota was awarded best CSR score by ethical quotation company Covalence in 2009 and Sony won the Sustainability Excellence Award by the Global Environmental Forum in 2006. However, only the Komatsu and Panasonic annual reports make a clear and direct reference to CSR. Furthermore, in the case of Sumitomo Chemical, they have reported on CSR for over a decade, have a well-respected and communicated development programme that operates and is increasingly run from Tanzania. It has been a member of 'global norms' for some time too. This is largely a result of being a member of an industry that has a high public profile and whose members globally have long reported and thought about their corporate responsibility. These results compare with the general trading company/international firms that have a more limited history of reporting on CSR. For example, Itochu started their CSR reports in 2006 and Sumitomo in 2005. International firms also highlight Japanese CSR accolades rather than global awards won.

Similarly, international firms and global MNCs studied here both high-lighted decision-making that occurred with home country bias with top-down, centralised decision-making, at the expense of subsidiary country sensitivities. For example, most of the MNCs focus mainly on CSR that takes place in Japan rather than in subsidiary countries. Panasonic, Itochu, Sumitomo and Komatsu concentrate more on reporting CSR occurring in Japan than they do in South Africa and Tanzania. For instance, both types of companies highlight the impor-tance of Japanese heritage to the way they approach CSR. They universally pay tribute to the history and heritage of the organisation and its influence on CSR. Itochu is a good example of a company that really emphasises heritage and Japanese/local tradition. The company ethos of 'sampo yoshi' is defined as the 'tradition of ITOCHU that we always ask ourselves whether a business is truly good for society'. Furthermore, many of the companies largely monitor and command the CSR decision-making process in Tanzania or South Africa. This is evidenced from the interviews—and noted in Table 1—for Panasonic, Itochu, Sumitomo, Sumitomo Chemical and to an extent, Toyota. This is particularly the case in ensuring that head office priorities outweigh those of subsidiary opera-tions in South Africa. For instance, Sony and Komatsu either refuse to be graded according to their CSR impact (required through South African legislation) or receive such low grades that they are largely barred from public procurement contracts (see for example du Toit, 2008).

Despite these findings, there are examples whereby international firms and global MNCs do not conform to stereotype; some—especially Toyota—also display traits that come close to being transnational. Both types of companies operating in South Africa have shown sensitivity to issues that have emerged from the local South African context. Komatsu highlights a specific South African initiative that exists with a partner, DenRon, which is a Community Development Centre that supports education to improve skills required for the quarry and materials industry near its base in Plettenberg. Toyota relates CSR to South African domestic CSR principles and wider narratives on CSR; educa-tion has been a core focus for decades. Furthermore, global firms do not always conform to type, highlighting the way that local stakeholders are included in the decision-making process. For example, Komatsu, Toyota and Sony have host country staff responsible for the implementation of local CSR.

Of the seven MNCs reviewed, Toyota and Komatsu in some ways deviate most from their expected typologies. Toyota in contrast, displays some transnational traits despite an intransigent managerial structure. Not only does it produce

Toyota region-specific reports but it has a wealth of customised CSR initiatives that run in a semi-autonomous fashion in its subsidiary countries including South Africa. Komatsu come close to operating on multidomestic lines because of their tendency to work on a 50/50 basis with local companies when they work around the world and receive poor ratings for 'global' CSR priorities such as efforts regarding human rights issues (CanPan, 2008).

Conclusion: organisational geographies in a Japanese context

This article originated from a view expressed in management literature that Japanese companies still display distinct, home-country approaches to strategy (and therefore categorised as an international firm approach) even when trading across multiple continents. This led me to explore the concept of organisational geographies and how companies are expected to act when geographical and organisational cultures and typologies (and even typographies) are woven together. I believe that the appreciation of viewing organisations (and the way strategies are created) is rather limited in academic literature and across business in general. So, this article highlights the concept of 'organisational geographies' as a tool that can help shed light on the geographical and organisational cultures that help shape the strategy and practice of CSR. It does so by recognising that geography (often meaning culture) alone cannot explain how corporate responsibility is strategised as other influences are clearly also important (Blowfield and Murray, 2008: 181). The contribution of the article is the refinement of different conceptualisations of geographical influences on how corporate responsibility is approached by MNCs and thus helps illuminate the implication and opportunities for management studies and corporate citizenship. It therefore adds to the nascent literature on the organisational geographies that help influence the strategy of CSR.

This article highlighted five conceptualisations that frame how organisational geographies might shape the CSR strategy of MNCs. All of the companies studied relate to at least one of these geographies:

▶ Itochu—an international firm

▶ Komatsu—mixture of global shareholder and multidomestic

▶ Panasonic—global stakeholder

▶ Sony—mixture of global shareholder and multidomestic

▶ Toyota—transnational

Unsurprisingly, there is evidence that shows that the **international firm** and **global stakeholder firm** in particular conform to type. Both display centralised decision-making often with limited local (host country) input. CSR priorities relate to Japanese 'norms' for international firms and there is a stress on global norms for global firms. International firms display more limited commitment to CSR; compared to global stakeholder firms that tend to employ many more, have a longer public commitment to CSR and a decision-making system that reports to senior executive staff. Similarly, Toyota as a probable example of a transnational company comes closest to operating what might be regarded to be a transnational CSR operation—due in part to its length and extent of operation in South Africa.

Of course, MNCs often display more than one trait of 'strategic spatiality' at the same time. For instance, a company can be associated with an overarching global firm strategy but also be regarded as working along multidomestic lines when implementing CSR. Furthermore, approaches to strategy alter depending on the evolutionary life cycle of the MNC. These caveats are important to note when considering the results. Furthermore, there are times when international firms do show signs of global norms. Global stakeholder firms have made a virtue of their Japanese heritage, which shows the historical commitment to CSR. That many of the traits (especially from the international firm and global firm view) are evident from the findings should not be surprising given the polysemic identity of Japan, incorporating both traditional values and the embracement of a form of Westernisation. What this shows is that change to CSR in Japan is incremental; the fastest pace comes unsurprisingly from those who have expanded/operated the most internationally and with the longest history of operating outside Japan and Asia.

References

Bartlett, C.A., and Ghoshal, S. (1998) *Managing Across Borders: The Transnational Solution*, Cambridge, Mass, USA: Harvard University Press.

Blowfield, M., and Murray, A. (2008) *Corporate Responsibility—a critical introduction*, Oxford: Oxford University Press.

CanPan. (2008). CSR Company Information rating and comparison. Accessed from http://canpan.info/csr_info_en, accessed November 2009.

Chandler, A.D. (1962) *Strategy Structure*, Cambridge, Mass (USA): MIT Press.

Coe, N.M., Dicken, P., and Hess, M. (2008) Global production networks: realizing the potential. *Journal of Economic Geography*, 8: 271-295.

Collinson, S., and Rugman, A.M. (2008) The regional nature of Japanese multinational business. *Journal of International Business Studies*, 39: 1-16.

Dicken, P. (2005) Tangled webs: transnational production networks and regional integration, *SPACES Working Paper 2005-04*. Geography, University of Marburg.

Dicken, P. (2007) *Global Shift: Mapping the Changing Contours of the World Economy*. London: Sage.

Du Toit, C. (2008) Sony defends SABC deal, accessed from http://www.itweb.co.za/index.php?option=com_content&view+art, accessed 13 July 2010.

The Economist (2009) Toyota Slips Up. *The Economist*. 10 December.

Fukukawa, K., and Moon, J. (2004) A Japanese Model of Corporate Social Responsibility. *Journal of Corporate Citizenship*, 14: 45-59.

Hughes, A., Buttle, M., and Wrigley, N. (2007) Organisational geographies of corporate responsibility: a UK-US comparison of retailers' ethical trading initiatives. *Journal of Economic Geography*, 7: 491-513.

KPMG. (2008) *KPMG International Survey of Corporate Responsibility Reporting 2008.*

Lewin, A., Sakano, T., Stephens, C., and Victor, B. (1995) Corporate Citizenship in Japan: Survey Results from Japanese firms. *Journal of Business Ethics,* 14: 83-101.

MacIntyre, A. (1984) *After Virtue: A Study in Moral Theory,* University of Notre Dame Press, 2nd edn.

Morgan, G., Kelly, B., Sharpe, D., and Whitley, R. (2003) Global managers and Japanese multinationals: internationalization and management in Japanese financial institutions. *International Journal of Human Resource Management.* 14: 389-407.

Ooko, S. (2009). Tanzania to Host first Corporate Social Responsibility Day. Accessed from http://www.greenbusinessafrica.com/2009/05/13/tanzania-to-hold-first-corporate-social-responsibility-day/, accessed 19 July 2010.

Ouchi, W.G. (1980). Markets, bureaucracies and clans. *Administrative Science Quarterly.* 25: 129-141.

Palmer, M., and O'Kane, P. (2007) Strategy as practice: interactive governance spaces and the corporate strategies of retail transnationals. *Journal of Economic Geography,* 7: 515-535.

Parsons, W. (1995) *Public Policy: An introduction to the theory and practice of policy analysis,* London: Edward Elgar.

Pascale, R.T., and Athos, A.G. (1981) The art of Japanese Management. *Business Horizons,* 24: 83-85.

Pettigrew, A. M. (2009) Corporate Responsibility in Strategy. In: *Mainstreaming Corporate Responsibility,* editors Smith, N.C., and Lenssen, G., pp. 12-20.

Porter, M.E. (2000) Location, Competition and Economic Development: Local Clusters in a Global Economy, *Economic Development Quarterly,* 14: 15-34.

Segal-Horn, S., and Faulkner, D. (1999) *The Dynamics of International Strategy.* London: Thomson.

Taka, I. (1997) Business Ethics in Japan, *Journal of Business Ethics,* 16: 14, 1499-1508.

Tanimoto, K. (2004). Changes in the market society and corporate social responsibility. Asian Business & Management, 3(2), 151-172.

West, A. (2006) Theorising South Africa's Corporate Governance, *Journal of Business Ethics,* 68: 433-448.

About the Journal of Corporate Citizenship

THE JOURNAL OF CORPORATE CITIZENSHIP (*JCC*) is a multidisciplinary peer-reviewed journal that focuses on integrating theory about corporate citizenship with management practice. It provides a forum in which the tensions and practical realities of making corporate citizenship real can be addressed in a reader-friendly, yet conceptually and empirically rigorous format.

JCC aims to publish *the best ideas integrating the theory and practice of corporate citizenship in a format that is readable, accessible, engaging, interesting and useful* for readers in its already wide audience in business, consultancy, government, NGOs and academia. It encourages practical, theoretically sound, and (when relevant) empirically rigorous manuscripts that address real-world implications of corporate citizenship in global and local contexts. Topics related to corporate citizenship can include (but are not limited to): corporate responsibility, stakeholder relationships, public policy, sustainability and environment, human and labour rights/issues, governance, accountability and transparency, globalisation, small and medium-sized enterprises (SMEs) as well as multinational firms, ethics, measurement, and specific issues related to corporate citizenship, such as diversity, poverty, education, information, trust, supply chain management, and problematic or constructive corporate/human behaviours and practices.

In addition to articles linking the theory and practice of corporate citizenship, *JCC* also encourages innovative or creative submissions (for peer review). Innovative submissions can highlight issues of corporate citizenship from a critical perspective, enhance practical or conceptual understanding of corporate citizenship, or provide new insights or alternative perspectives on the realities of corporate citizenship in today's world. Innovative submissions might include: critical perspectives and controversies, photography, essays, poetry, drama, reflections, and other innovations that help bring corporate citizenship to life for management practitioners and academics alike.

JCC welcomes contributions from researchers and practitioners involved in any of the areas mentioned above. Manuscripts should be written so that they are comprehensible to an intelligent reader, avoiding jargon, formulas and extensive methodological treatises wherever possible. They should use examples and illustrations to highlight the ideas, concepts and practical implications of the ideas being presented. Theory is important and necessary; but theory—with the empirical research and conceptual work that supports theory—needs to be balanced by integration into practices to stand the tests of time and usefulness. *JCC* aims to be the premier journal to publish articles on corporate citizenship that accomplish this integration of theory and practice. We want the journal to be read as much by executives leading corporate citizenship as it is by academics seeking sound research and scholarship.

JCC appears quarterly and includes peer-reviewed papers by leading writers, with occasional reviews, case studies and think-pieces. A key feature is the 'Turning Points' section. Turning Points are commentaries, controversies, new ideas, essays and insights that aim to be provocative and engaging, raise the important issues of the day and provide observations on what is too new yet to be the subject of empirical and theoretical studies. *JCC* continues to produce occasional issues dedicated to a single theme. These have included 'Story Telling: Beyond the Academic Article—Using Fiction, Art and Literary Techniques to Communicate', 'Sustainable Luxury', 'Business–NGO Partnerships', 'Creating Global Citizens and Responsible Leadership', 'Responsible Investment in Emerging Markets', 'The Positive Psychology of Sustainable Enterprise', 'Textiles, Fashion and Sustainability', 'Designing Management Education', 'Managing by Design' and 'Innovative Stakeholder.

EDITORS

General Editor:

Malcolm McIntosh, Asia-Pacific Centre for Sustainable Enterprise, Griffith Business School, Australia; email: jcc@griffith.edu.au.

Regional Editor:

North American Editor: Sandra Waddock, Professor of Management, Boston College, Carroll School of Management, Senior Research Fellow, Center for Corporate Citizenship, Chestnut Hill, MA 02467 USA; tel: +1 617 552 0477; fax: +1 617 552 0433; email: waddock@bc.edu

Notes for Contributors

SUBMISSIONS

All content should be submitted via online submission. For more information see the journal homepage at www.greenleaf-publishing.com/jcc.

The form gives prompts for the required information and asks authors to submit the full text of the paper, including the title, author name and author affiliation, as a Word attachment. **Abstract and keywords will be completed via the online submission and are not necessary on the attachment.**

As part of the online submission authors will be asked to tick a box to state they have read and adhere to the Greenleaf–GSE Copyright Guidelines and have permission to publish the paper, including all figures, images, etc which have been taken from other sources. It is the author's responsibility to ensure this is correct.

In order to be able to distribute papers published in Greenleaf journals, we need signed transfer of copyright from the authors. We are committed to a liberal and fair approach to copyright and accessibility, and do not restrict authors' rights to reuse their own work for personal use or in an institutional repository.

A brief autobiographical note should be supplied at the end of the paper including:

- Full name
- Affiliation
- Email address
- Full international contact details

Please supply (via online submission) an **abstract outlining the title, purpose, methodology and main findings.** It's worth considering that, as your paper will be located and read online, the quality of your abstract will determine whether readers go on to access your full paper. We recommend you place particular focus on the impact of your research on further research, practice or society. What does your paper contribute?

In addition, please provide up to **six descriptive keywords.**

FORMATTING YOUR PAPER

Headings should be short and in bold text, with a clear and consistent hierarchy.

Please identify **Notes or Endnotes** with consecutive numbers, enclosed in square brackets and listed at the end of the article.

Figures and other images should be submitted as .jpeg (.jpg) or .tif files and be of a high quality. Please number consecutively with Arabic numerals and mark clearly within the body of the text where they should be placed.

If images are not the original work of the author, it is the author's responsibility to obtain written consent from the copyright holder to them being used. Authors will be asked to confirm this is the case by ticking the box on the online submission to say they have read and understood the Greenleaf–GSE copyright policy. Images which are neither the authors' own work, nor are accompanied by such permission will not be published.

Tables should be included as part of the manuscript, with relevant captions.

Supplementary data can be appended to the article, using the form and should follow the same formatting rules as the main text.

References to other publications should be complete and in Harvard style, e.g. (Jones, 2011) for one author, (Jones and Smith, 2011) for two authors and (Jones *et al.*, 2011) for more than two authors. A full reference list should appear at the end of the paper.

- For **books:** Surname, Initials (year), *Title of Book*, Publisher, Place of publication.
  e.g. Author, J. (2011), *This is my book*, Publisher, New York, NY.
- For **book chapters:** Surname, Initials (year), "Chapter title", Editor's Surname, Initials, *Title of Book*, Publisher, Place of publication, pages (if known).
- For **journals:** Surname, Initials (year), "Title of article", *Title of Journal*, volume, number, pages.
- For **conference proceedings:** Surname, Initials (year), "Title of paper", in Surname, Initials (Ed.), Title of published proceeding which may include place and date(s) held, Publisher, Place of publication, Page numbers.
- For **newspaper articles:** Surname, Initials (year) (if an author is named), "Article title", *Newspaper*, date, pages.
- For **images:**
  Where image is from a printed source—as for books but with the page number on which the image appears.
  Where image is from an online source—Surname, Initials (year), Title, Available at, Date accessed.
  Other images—Surname, Initials (year), Title, Name of owner (person or institution) and location for viewing.

▶ **To discuss ideas for contributions**, please contact the General Editor: Malcolm McIntosh, Asia-Pacific Centre for Sustainable Enterprise, Griffith Business School, Australia; email: jcc@griffith.edu.au.